D1630527

CHARITY TAXATION
A DEFINITIVE GUIDE

Leeds Metropolitan University

17 0377665 5

CHARITY TAXATION
A DEFINITIVE GUIDE

Adrian J. L. Randall FCA BSc(Econ)
Stephen Williams BA MPhil ACA

JORDANS
2001

Published by
Jordan Publishing Limited
21 St Thomas Street
Bristol BS1 6JS

Copyright © Jordan Publishing Limited 2001

All rights reserved. No part of this publication may be reproduced, stored in a
retrieval system, or transmitted in any way or by any means, including photocopying
or recording, without the written permission of the copyright holder, application for
which should be addressed to the publisher.

British Library Cataloguing-in-Publication Data
A catalogue record for this book is available from the British Library.

ISBN 0 85308 635 4

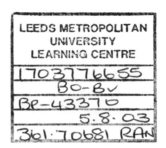

LEEDS METROPOLITAN
UNIVERSITY
LEARNING CENTRE

1703776655
BO-BV
BP-43370
5.8.03
361.70681 RAN

Typeset by Mendip Communications Ltd, Frome, Somerset
Printed in Great Britain by MPG Books Ltd, Bodmin, Cornwall

ACKNOWLEDGEMENTS

Thanks are due to the students on the South Bank University Diploma/MSC in Charity Finance for their helpful suggestions on the practical issues relating to charities and on the lecture notes which form the main core of this book.

We would also like to thank Jim Pinder, VAT Partner, BDO Stoy Hayward, who kindly offered comments on Chapters 9 and 10; Mike Sutherland, Tax Manager, BDO Stoy Hayward, who kindly offered comments on Chapter 6; and Jennifer Randall for all the assistance she gave, particularly in typing up most of the book.

Sole responsibility for the contents of the book lies with the authors.

PREFACE

In writing this book, our intention has been to provide a readable practical guide to an area which, unfortunately, is one of the most complex in the UK tax system; that is the relationship between charities and the various taxes which make up that system. The misfortune is that many charities do not have the necessary technical resources and we hope, therefore, through this book to:

- increase the level of tax awareness amongst those people who work in the charity sector;
- highlight the danger areas;
- show when it might be necessary to draw on professional assistance;
- enable the reader to contribute positively to the development of the tax policy of his or her organisation.

However, the book is not just a guide to the complexities of the rules. The Review of Charity Taxation announced in July 1997 promised much and we have attempted to highlight in detail the changes which have been introduced. Indeed, we believe that many of the pitfalls described in our previous book *Charities and Taxation* (ICSA Publishing, 1995) have been removed and we are at last beginning to get somewhere towards 'crossing the minefield'. Nevertheless, problems still remain for charities in the field of taxation, not least when it comes to the issues of VAT, and we hope that this book will provide some practical solutions.

For ease of reference, the masculine gender has been used throughout and should be read as including the feminine.

ADRIAN RANDALL
STEPHEN WILLIAMS
Norfolk and London
January 2001

CONTENTS

TABLE OF CASES

References are to paragraph numbers.

TABLE OF STATUTES

References are to paragraph numbers, addendum to chapter 10, and Appendix.

TABLE OF STATUTORY INSTRUMENTS

References are to paragraph numbers.

TABLE OF EUROPEAN MATERIAL

References are to paragraph numbers.

TABLE OF OTHER MATERIAL

References are to paragraph numbers.

TABLE OF ABBREVIATIONS

AC	Appeal cases
ACT	Advance corporation tax
ATC	*Annotated Tax Cases*
AMR	Authorised Mileage Rates
CA	Contributions Agency
CGS	Capital goods scheme
CGT	Capital gains tax
CTT	Capital transfer tax
CIR	Commissioners of the Inland Revenue
CTRG	Charities' Tax Reform Group
ECCVAT	European Charities Commission on VAT
ESC	Extra-statutory concession
EU	European Union
FA 1969	Finance Act 1969
FA 1972	Finance Act 1972
FA 1975	Finance Act 1975
FA 1976	Finance Act 1976
FA 1982	Finance Act 1982
FA 1985	Finance Act 1985
FA 1987	Finance Act 1987
FA 1999	Finance Act 1999
FA 2000	Finance Act 2000
GAYE	Give as you earn
ICAEW	Institute of Chartered Accountants in England and Wales
ICT	Income and corporation tax
ICTA 1988	Income and Corporation Taxes Act 1988
IEA	Institute of Economic Affairs
IHT	Inheritance tax
IHTA 1984	Inheritance Tax Act 1984
IR	Inland Revenue
IRC	Inland Revenue Commissioners
LGFA 1988 and 1992	Local Government Finance Acts 1988 and 1992
NIC	National Insurance contributions
PAYE	Pay as you earn
PCTCT	Profits chargeable to corporation tax
PET	Potentially exempt transfer
PSBR	Public sector borrowing requirement
SDRT	Stamp duty reserve tax

STC	*Simon's Tax Cases*
TC	*Tax Cases*
TCGA 1992	Taxation of Chargeable Gains Act 1992
UBR	Uniform business rate
VAT	Value added tax
VATA 1994	Value Added Tax Act 1994
VATTR	VAT *Tribunal Reports*

Chapter 1

INTRODUCTION

'Charities don't pay tax do they?'

Source unknown

1.1 MYTH AND REALITY

It is a commonly held belief that charities do not pay tax. If it were true then this would be a very short book. Although charities do not have blanket exemption from taxation,[1] reliefs are available against some taxes, but certain requirements have to be fulfilled before advantage can be taken of them. However, some taxes do not have exemptions for charities at all. It is, nevertheless, true to say that charities can enjoy a very favourable tax regime if the requirements are met, particularly in relation to direct taxes, and it is one of the main objectives of this book to highlight the requirements, and to point out the potential problems and to proffer some solutions. In doing so, we will also attempt to set out the tax reliefs available to donors when giving to charities. It is necessary to understand the difference between the two types of tax relief available: (1) to charities; and (2) to donors.

However, before we look in detail at the nature of the relationship between charity and taxation, it is worthwhile briefly to set the scene by providing some background to the UK tax system.

1.2 BACKGROUND

The UK tax system is a collection of rules and regulations designed to achieve certain objectives. Unfortunately, over time the rules often appear to lose contact with the objectives behind their introduction, and are often consolidated, producing baffling results. Once a rule becomes law then a deliberate effort is needed to change or remove it. In the highly pressured world of politics, it is often difficult to build up and sustain this effort when there are always more pressing issues to be dealt with. As a result, the rules remain long after the memory of why they were originally introduced has faded away.

---

1   There are various terms for the relaxation of the full rigour of the tax regime: exemption, relief and allowance. 'Exemption' means removal of a particular type of income from tax; 'relief' means a mechanism whereby an individual can mitigate his or her tax burden; and 'allowance' means a certain amount of tax-free income made available by the rules of the tax system.

It is often suggested that the UK tax system lacks logic and a unified construction. Taxation, because of its legal and political background, has little to do with economics. The tax system can, therefore seem more irrational than it is in reality when one considers the original purpose of a particular taxation rule. The effects, however, may be different from those originally intended, either because of poor parliamentary draftsmanship, or because the world has moved on to such an extent as to render the original purpose impossible to fulfil.

The way the rules of UK tax are set out and interpreted is primarily through statute law, as amended and consolidated from time to time, and then as interpreted by the courts. In this book, as we will consider in some detail the statutory provisions in relation to charity taxation, it is worthwhile considering the nature of basic tax law. The principal statutes in relation to the significant UK taxes are:

Income tax and corporation tax	Income and Corporation Taxes Act 1988 together with subsequent Finance Acts	ICTA 1988
Value added tax	Value Added Tax 1994, and statutory instruments, together with subsequent Finance Acts and EC Directives	VATA 1994
National Insurance	Social Security Contributions and Benefits Act 1992, and statutory instruments	
Capital gains tax	Taxation of Chargeable Gains Act 1992 and subsequent Finance Acts	TCGA 1992
Inheritance Tax	Inheritance Tax Act 1984 and subsequent Finance Acts	IHTA 1984
Business rates and council tax	Local Government Finance Acts 1988 and 1992	LGFA 1988 and 1992
Stamp duty	Stamp Act 1891 and subsequent Finance Acts	

Tax law, like any other law, needs to be interpreted and, to assist in this process, there are various rules led by the 'golden rule' whereby ordinary words in the statute are to be given their natural meanings as far as possible within the context in which they appear in the statute. The 'golden rule' has not always been observed and, in the charity context, it was most clearly not followed in the important *Pemsel* case. The case turned on the definition of the word 'charity' as it occurred in the Income Tax Acts of 1842 and 1853. In giving his judgment, Lord McNaghten said that the natural meaning of charity has 'not yet adequately been defined, and probably cannot be'. This particular case arose because the Inland Revenue attempted during the late 1880s to change the long-standing wide natural definition and restrict it to the relief of poverty only. Their attempt was unsuccessful.

1.3 OPERATING PRINCIPLES

In attempting the brief review, we will begin with a look at some of the operating principles behind three major taxes: (1) income and corporation tax; (2) capital gains tax; and (3) inheritance tax.

1.3.1 Income and corporation tax

If income is to be taxed, then it has to fall within one of the schedules of income tax. If income does not fall under any schedule then it is not recognised as taxable income. One example of this is where an individual gives a charity £100. If this is not given under a Gift Aid declaration then it is not income as recognised by the tax system in the charity's hands. If the individual Gift Aids the £100 then the amount becomes recognisable by the tax system and thus potentially taxable.

This system of schedules was introduced in 1803 and retained on the reintroduction of income tax in 1842. Historically, it was felt that one reason for dealing with income in this way was to assure early income tax payers that no single government office would know the full picture; a principle which has long been overtaken! There are particular rules for calculating tax for these schedules and they are mutually exclusive so that one type of income will not be taxed under more than one schedule. Charities' exemptions relate to specific schedules, therefore it is important to have a basic understanding of them.

However, one result of this doctrine is that anything which is not recognised as income must be capital and therefore not chargeable under income and corporation tax. The distinction between capital and revenue is one where case-law has provided operating principles to make the tax legislation work. Connected to this distinction is the question of whether income is the result of a trading activity or a one-off activity, and therefore taxable or not. The 'badges of trade' has evolved as a summary of the principles operating in this area. This is discussed in more detail in Chapter 4.

1.3.2 Capital gains tax

As we have seen, income and corporation tax does not recognise capital; therefore one of two other taxes comes into play here: capital gains tax (CGT) or inheritance tax (IHT). CGT aims to tax the difference between the disposal proceeds of an asset (which has not been disposed of as the result of trading) and its original cost. CGT does not tax gains as they accrue over the period of ownership, as the tax is only charged on the actual, or 'deemed' disposal. A deemed event is one where the law states that something has happened for tax purposes, which has not actually happened, ie where the title to the assets has not been transferred. One example of this, which we discuss in more detail in Chapter 5, is when a charity loses its charitable status. A disposal can include gifts, where title is transferred for free or below market value, in which case tax law inserts a deemed amount of proceeds, ie the market value, even though little or no consideration changes hands. Effectively, therefore, CGT is a gift tax.

1.3.3   Inheritance tax

IHT is chargeable on transfers of value. These occur when an individual, a trustee or certain companies controlled by an individual, as a result of giving away some of the property under their control, have reduced the value of their estates. IHT is aimed at gifts. However, most gifts, if made more than seven years before the death of the donor escape IHT, and are not included in the accumulation rule. As the biggest transfer of value usually occurs on an individual's death then IHT is chargeable, except where everything is left to the spouse. Currently (2000/2001), IHT is not chargeable on transfers up to a cumulative amount of £234,000, a figure which is reviewed annually in the Budget. However, if this limit is exceeded then additional transfers are potentially chargeable at the lifetime rate (currently 20%) in force when the transfer occurs. If death occurs within seven years, tax will be charged on that transfer at the full rate (currently 40%), subject to taper relief. If more than seven years elapse without death, the transfer will fall out of the accumulation rule. There is an annual exemption of £3,000 and additional relief for small gifts, ie below £250, made to any one person.

1.4   DEFINITION OF A CHARITY FOR TAX PURPOSES

Not all voluntary or non profit-making organisations are charities. Tax legislation defines a charity as 'any body of persons or trust established for charitable purposes only', but does not define charitable purposes. To find out what are considered 'charitable purposes', one has to go back to an Act of 1601 and a line of court decisions which have further developed and extended the definition.

One particular court decision already referred to[1] set out four general headings for charitable purposes, which have stood the test of time. These are:

(1) the relief of poverty;
(2) the advancement of education;
(3) the advancement of religion;
(4) other purposes of a charitable nature beneficial to the community not falling under any of the other headings.

Where a charity's purposes fall within one of the first three categories above, they are assumed to be charitable and for the benefit of the community unless it

---

1   *Pemsel v IRC* (1891) 3 TC 80.

is shown otherwise. But in the fourth category, a purpose must be shown to benefit the community in a way which the law regards as charitable. A purpose contrary to public policy cannot be for the benefit of the community and not only will it not be charitable, but it will be void. Charitable status will not be accorded if the purposes:

– contain an over element of self-help;
– are not exclusively charitable;
– are substantially political;
– involve profit distribution.

The Income and Corporation Taxes Act 1988 (ICTA 1988) defines a charity as 'any body of persons or trust established for charitable purposes only', but that is only for the purposes of ICTA 1988, ss 505, 506 and 761(6).

A wide range of purposes have been accepted in the past as charitable, which means that similar purposes of new organisations will also be accepted as charitable. These include:

– the provision of land and buildings for public use, such as recreation grounds and community halls;
– the conservation of the national heritage;
– the relief of sick, mentally or physically handicapped, disabled or old people, the rehabilitation of offenders or drug abusers and similar purposes;
– the care of animals needing protection;
– the provision of recreation facilities, so long as they are in the interests of social welfare and aim to improve the conditions of life for the people for whom the facilities are intended;
– providing sports facilities open to the public.

All these purposes are limited and defined by decisions of the courts and advice should be taken before setting up a new organisation. The Charity Commissioners will give a preliminary ruling on whether proposed purposes are charitable before an organisation is actually formed and a formal application for charitable status is made.

Some purposes are not charitable and charities are barred from involvement in these activities. They include:

– political campaigning and pressure group activities;
– permanent trading unless for the purposes of carrying out its charitable objectives (but see Chapter 4 for how a charity can benefit from a separate trading company);
– arrangements where the individuals running the charity benefit personally.

A charity receives its status by virtue of its objectives and not its legal form. Therefore, a charity can be set up, for example as a trust, a limited company, an unincorporated association, a friendly society, a housing association or by an

Act of Parliament. A trust is normally used where one or more people want to settle property which will be used permanently for charitable purposes. A limited company normally will be incorporated as a company limited by guarantee without share capital. In simple terms, an unincorporated association is a club whose members aim to achieve a common charitable purpose.

A charity must have a governing document and the nature of this depends on the legal form of the charity. People who wish to form a charity are advised to engage a solicitor to prepare the governing document, although some model governing documents exist (examples are obtainable from the Charity Commission).

The tax legislation does not insist that a charity is registered with the Charity Commissioners before it qualifies for tax exemptions. However, in practice a body in England or Wales (the Charity Commissioners do not cover Scotland and Northern Ireland) with an annual income in excess of £1,000 must normally be registered unless it is a type of charity that does not have to register, eg exempt or excepted.[1]

However, the registration of a charity with the Charity Commission is an important first step to acceptance by the Inland Revenue as being eligible for tax concessions. The second and third steps are to show that the income can be exempt and that the expenditure qualifies (see further, Chapter 2).

The Charity Commissioners may consult the Inland Revenue during the registration process as the Inland Revenue is entitled to object to the registration of an organisation. However, a charity must still apply separately to the Charity Title section of the Inland Revenue's Financial Intermediaries and Claims Office (FICO) for tax exempt status, although this will normally be just a formality for a registered charity. The application should include a copy of the charity's governing document and most recent accounts, if any.

Although Scotland has its own charity law, currently being revised, the House of Lords held in *Pemsel* that the English law of charities has to be regarded for income tax purposes only as part of the law of Scotland. This also applies to Northern Ireland.

The people in charge of running a charity are called trustees in the legislation, although they may go under other names in the charity's governing document. For example, a charity which is established as a company limited by guarantee has directors who are therefore the trustees.

Trustees of a charity have the duty to ensure that its income is used only for its charitable purposes and that it complies with all the legal requirements imposed on charities. The Charities Acts 1992 and 1993 made many changes to the law relating to charities, which came into effect in several stages. Their provisions cover charity accounts, charity documents, annual returns to the Charity Commissioners, public collections, the sale of land owned by charities

---

1   See further, Charities Act 1993.

and many other areas. The Charity Commissioners have published a guide to the law, *A Guide to the Charities Acts 1992 & 1993*, which is very clearly written, and charity trustees and administrators are recommended to read it.

1.5 TAXES AND CHARITIES

Let us now look at the interaction between the three main types of legal structure by which charities set themselves up and the four main taxes (income/corporation tax, CGT and IHT), before tax mechanisms are taken into account, since we need to know what will happen if, for some reason, an exemption is not available.

1.5.1 Trusts and income tax

First, let us look at trusts and income tax. One of the main reasons for the development of trusts has been the avoidance of taxation. From a tax point of view, the simple idea behind a trust is that the individual who gives property to a trust is no longer the owner of that property and so cannot be taxed as though he were. Originally, the response of the tax authorities was to claim that the income was the individual's; subsequently, they claimed that it was the income of the trust's beneficiaries. Since the trust owns the trust property and is entitled to any income which arises from that property, the Inland Revenue will assess the trust on any taxable income arising. Unfortunately, the trust itself cannot claim personal allowances because it is not an 'individual'.

The tax liability arising on any particular income, less expenses specific to raising that income, will be calculated in accordance with the rules of the schedule into which it falls. For example, where a trust carries on a trade, then expenses incurred wholly and exclusively for the purposes of that trade will be deductible for tax purposes. Trusts are charged on their income at basic rate, currently 22% (2000/2001). The lower rate of 10% and higher rate of 40% do not apply to trusts because they are not individuals.

1.5.2 Trusts and CGT

Secondly, we look at how CGT impinges upon trusts. To start with a tax 'repetition', CGT is charged on the chargeable disposal of chargeable assets by a chargeable person. Chargeable disposal we referred to earlier; chargeable assets include all assets except motor cars, gilt-edged stocks and assets with a predictable life of less than fifty years, such as a television. An individual's home is a chargeable asset but the gain is exempted if it is one's principal private residence. A trust may own a home which it can allow a beneficiary to use. If the conditions of s 225 of the Taxation of Chargeable Gains Act 1992 are met, it would give rise on disposal to a tax-free gain.

The annual CGT exemption is £7,200 for the 2000/2001 tax year (£7,100 for 1999/2000). The exemption cannot be carried forward and it would be lost if not used in the tax year. Most trusts are entitled to an annual exemption of half the above amount, ie £3,600 for 2000/2001. With effect from 6 April 2000, gains are charged at 10% where, when added to taxable income, they amount to less than the starting rate limit (£1,520 for 2000/2001); 20% where they amount to less than the basic rate (£28,400 for 2000/2001); and 40% where they exceed that limit. There are major changes to the CGT taper rules which apply for disposals of business assets on or after 6 April 2000.

Gains arising on the disposal of an interest in a UK trust are not generally chargeable to CGT. This exemption has been exploited by individuals to sell assets tax-free to third parties. From 21 March 2000, where an interest in a settlor-interested trust is disposed of for consideration, the trust assets to which the interest relates are deemed to be disposed of and reacquired by the trustees at their market value. Any resultant gains will not qualify for gift holdover relief and will be chargeable on the settlor under the normal provisions. This rule will also apply to property forming part of a settlement in which the settlor had an interest at any time in the two previous tax years.

Where a charity makes a capital profit, for example from selling investments, it is exempt from CGT provided that the profit is used for its charitable purposes only (TCGA 1992, s 256). This is dealt with in more detail in Chapter 5.

1.5.3   Trusts and IHT

Thirdly, we see how inheritance tax affects trusts. IHT's impact on trusts depends on how the trust is set up and whether it is a trust with an interest in possession, eg a trust with a life tenant. If there is no interest in possession then it will be treated for IHT purposes very differently, assuming it is not a special trust, such as a children's accumulation and maintenance trust, a pension fund, an employees trust or a charitable trust. Each of these have special treatment. This will be discussed further in Chapter 5.

The creation of an interest in possession trust during the settlor's lifetime is a potentially exempt transfer, thus no IHT is payable unless the settlor dies within seven years. If the trust was created on death, then IHT would have been paid primarily by the deceased's personal representatives, or if they failed to pay it, the beneficiary who has the interest in possession. In IHT terms, the life tenant of the trust is the owner of the assets. On that person's death the assets of the trust will be included in the estate and taxed accordingly at the death rates.

The treatment of a trust without an interest in possession differs because the trust is the taxable entity, as it owns the assets. Tax may therefore be payable if the transfer exceeds the cumulative total of chargeable transfers already made. This is of relevance, chiefly to determine whether or not the chargeable transfer exceeds the threshold of £234,000, as the tax charged will always be at lifetime rates, currently 20%. Since the trust is not an individual and effectively cannot die, the death rate of 40% will never apply.

The next occasion of charge will be on the tenth anniversary of the creation of the trust when its assets are deemed to be transferred, added to the cumulative transfer and charged at 20% if they are over the threshold. This anniversary charge will be levied every ten years. Other occasions of charge occur when trust property is passed to a beneficiary, for instance, when a discretionary trust hands over some of the assets to a selected beneficiary. Again, the tax is payable by the trustees. The annual exemption of £3,000 does not apply to such trusts, so tax could be payable whenever the trustees exercise their discretion, except when they make transfers to charities, which are exempt.

All outright gifts to charities, whether by will or during lifetime, are exempt without limit from IHT. The main value of this exemption is for gifts made by a will, as all gifts made during lifetime are in any case exempt provided that the donor lives for seven years after the gift.

A charity that takes the form of a trust is exempt from the ten-yearly charge to IHT that can arise for other trusts, provided that the property is held for charitable purposes only. However, IHT is payable where property is held on a temporary charitable trust in the following circumstances:

- where the property stops being held for charitable purposes, unless the reason for it leaving the trust is because it is being applied for a charitable purpose elsewhere;
- where the trustees do something that reduces the value of the property held by the trust, except making a gift for charitable purposes.

However, there are several instances in the circumstances shown above in which no tax arises. The main ones are where the value of trust property is reduced because of the payment of costs or expenses connected with the property, or where no gratuitous benefit to anyone else is intended.

Where a charge to IHT does arise, the amount payable is a variable percentage of the amount by which the value of the property within the trust has been reduced as a result of the event referred to above. If the trust itself pays the IHT (rather than the recipient of the property), then the amount of tax must be added to the reduction in the value of the trust's property. For example, if the value of property in the trust is reduced by £20,000 before IHT is paid and the rate of tax is 20%, then if the trust pays the tax its liability will be £5,000 (20% of £25,000).

The rate of tax depends on how long the property has been held on charitable trust and is a maximum of 30% where the property has been held for 50 years or more. Charities formed as limited companies or unincorporated associations cannot be charged IHT.

Where a charity is not a trust then it will be either a company limited by guarantee or otherwise, or an unincorporated association. It would be useful to be clear about the principles underlying the tax regime for these entities since many charities operate their trading activities within a separate limited company.

1.5.4   Companies and corporation tax

Companies, whether limited by shares or guarantee, and unincorporated associations pay corporation tax on their trading profits and on any chargeable gains they make. Chargeable gains are calculated in the same way as for individuals but without an annual exemption. Profits are calculated in accordance with tax rules, so each source is taxed according to the rules for the appropriate schedule; for example, rental income under Schedule A, or trading profits under the rules for Schedule D Case I.

A major difference between income tax and corporation tax is that because the company is a separate legal entity, the remuneration of those who direct it is an allowable expense when they are employees. Payments to the shareholders, chiefly dividends, are not allowable. However, one can be a director and a shareholder at the same time, thus ensuring that one's own remuneration is allowable for tax. Of course, since charitable companies, which are normally limited by guarantee rather than by shares, cannot employ the directors, as they are effectively the trustees of the charity, this is only relevant to non-charitable companies.

Another difference is that corporation tax is charged on a current year basis on the company's profits for the financial year. The financial year runs from 1 April to 31 March, and so if there are different rates of corporation tax in two financial years, the profits of the accounting year have to be apportioned, unless the accounting year coincides with the financial year. In recent years, this has not been necessary because the main corporation tax rate has remained at 30%. The rule remains relevant for calculating 'small companies rate', which is at 20%, and depends upon whether the level of taxable profit earned by the company is below £300,000 for an accounting year.

On 1 April 2000, a new starting rate of corporation tax of 10% was introduced. From that date, companies' profits are taxed as follows:

Taxable Profit	Rate of Corporation Tax (on profits in band)
£0–£10,000	10.0%
£10,001–£50,000	22.5%
£50,001–£300,000	20.0%
£300,001–£1,500,000	32.5%
above £1,500,000	30.0%

Although a donation to a national charity would not be allowable against the Schedule D Case I profit, it can be deducted as a charge if made via Gift Aid (see Chapter 5).

1.6   TAXATION REVIEW

In the first Labour Budget of July 1997, the Chancellor of the Exchequer, Gordon Brown, announced a Government review of charity taxation. The review was to be focused on VAT, but charities were told that they could also submit their comments on the effects of direct taxes and business rates by the deadline of 1 December 1997. A consultation document was to be published in the spring of 1998.

The consultation document eventually appeared in March 1999. Charities were given just five months, until 31 August 1999, to respond to the consultation document which had taken the Government some sixteen months to produce. Any dissatisfaction with the deadline for comments was increased by the realisation that the main emphasis had switched from VAT rationalisation to a review of charitable giving. Charities responded to the consultation document in vast numbers, spearheaded by the Charities' Tax Reform Group (CTRG), whose submission included some 88 proposals in a very well thought-out 41-page report. These specific CTRG proposals covered the whole range of issues raised by the consultation document but most importantly urged the Government to reconsider the VAT position of charities and take all steps in its power to lift this obstacle to an increase in voluntary and charitable activity across the UK.

LEEDS METROPOLITAN UNIVERSITY LEARNING CENTRE

It was not until 28 October 1999 that HM Treasury issued a press release entitled 'Charities are losing out on tax breaks'. This was followed very quickly by the Chancellor's Pre-Budget Report of 9 November. Although this did not deal directly very much with charities, there followed a raft of other press releases from the Inland Revenue, HM Customs and Excise and HM Treasury which announced a package of measures to improve giving to charities, reduce the impact of VAT and simplify the administration. All these improvements and changes were then scheduled to come into effect from April 2000, following the introduction of primary legislation wherever this was deemed necessary.

Not surprisingly, not everything that had been asked for by the charity sector was included in the Pre-Budget Report. Nevertheless it was probably fair to say that the Pre-Budget Report did highlight the introduction of a totally new way of tax-efficient giving. However, the Government left it to charities to increase donations and boost their income by offering greater tax incentives for doing so and claimed that the change in Gift Aid would be worth £300 million to the sector alone.

On 21 February 2000, one month before Budget Day, the draft legislation for 'Getting Britain Giving' was published. In a press release accompanying the documentation, the Economic Secretary, Melanie Johnson, was reported as saying:

> 'The Government values the significant contribution which charities have made in working with the Inland Revenue on the details of the measures contained in the draft legislation.'

The Government felt that the major proposals were:

–   the abolition of the £250 minimum limit for donations in the Gift Aid scheme so that tax relief will apply to any donation, large or small, regular or one-off;

–   the facility to join the Gift Aid scheme by phone or internet;

–   the abolition of the £1,200 maximum ceiling on Payroll Giving through the pay packet;

–   a 10% supplement on all donations to charities through Payroll Giving for three years;

–   a new income tax relief for gifts of listed shares and securities;

–   more exemptions for small trading and fundraising activities.

The Budget on 21 March 2000, therefore, had a few surprises as far as charities were concerned, but generally confirmed what had been forecast earlier.

1.7   VAT

Value added tax (VAT) is a very important tax from charities' point of view because of its relative lack of reliefs and the high cost of irrecoverable VAT. It is also a very different tax from the direct taxes discussed earlier. Rather than discuss its general operation here, we have devoted a chapter to general concepts (Chapter 9), and then another chapter to show how it affects charities (Chapter 10).

1.8   CONCLUSION

The remainder of this book follows a logical form. Chapter 2 describes the development of income tax charity reliefs and how they operate. Chapter 3 is concerned with tax-efficient giving to charity and reliefs for donor. Chapter 4, looks at the income and corporation tax problems associated with trading by charities. A review of capital taxes and reliefs for charities is dealt with in Chapter 5. Chapter 6 discusses the problems charities may encounter in relation to the taxation of their own employees, whilst Chapter 7 explores the relationship between local taxation and charities. Chapter 8 looks at two miscellaneous areas, namely taxation and disaster funds and charity reliefs from gambling taxes. Chapter 9 is a general discussion of the VAT system, and Chapter 10 looks into how this system affects charities. Finally, Chapter 11 reviews the current situation and assesses possible future developments.

Chapter 2

INCOME TAX RELIEF MECHANISMS

'By this it appears that Reason is not as Sense and Memory,
born with us; nor gotten by Experience onely'

Thomas Hobbes, *Leviathan*, 1651

2.1   INTRODUCTION

We will begin this chapter by considering the statutory provisions in detail. The principal sections of the Income and Corporation Taxes Act 1988 affecting charities are ss 505 and 506, which gather together most of the measures which have been introduced over the last 150 years. These sections contain the legislation dealing with the taxation of charities as such, but do not deal with the tax reliefs available to donors. The legislation dealing with these reliefs is scattered, partly because much of it was introduced after ICTA 1988.

2.2   ICTA 1988

2.2.1   Exemptions

Section 505(1) of ICTA 1988 is critical because it provides that exemptions are not granted automatically, but only on a claim: s 505(1)(c). This claim will need to be supported by evidence, or 'granted on proof before the Commissioners for Special Purposes', as the Income Tax Act 1842 put it. For the proof to be acceptable the claim must relate to income solely applicable for charitable purposes, and actually applied for charitable purposes.

Thus s 505 imposes a requirement on the charity to make a claim that it should be entitled to relief in a particular situation. Income tax is an annual tax, which means it has to be expressly voted for each year. In theory, this has the consequence in the Revenue's eyes that reliefs have to be proved annually also. Relief, once granted, will not automatically be renewed each year, although in practice if circumstances do not change there is a good chance that they will be. Problems may arise where the circumstances of the charity change; for example, the nature and size of the charity's income, the way in which money is spent, or the way the charity is organised. The Revenue may require additional assurance that the reliefs can still apply. If they are not satisfied, reliefs can be withdrawn.

The need for charities to claim for such exemptions conferred on the relevant department of the Revenue its original name, Claims Branch. The department is now part of the Financial Intermediaries and Claims Office (FICO), based in Bootle. The Revenue realised early on that it was better from their point of view that the treatment of charities should be standardised and that centralising their relations with the charity sector would secure this. Claims Branch originally dealt with the decision as to whether or not an organisation was charitable but this function is now carried out by the Charity Commission for England and Wales.

Section 505(1)(a) exempts rents or other receipts from rights over land, whether located in the UK or elsewhere. It is a requirement that all income exempted by s 505 must be applied for charitable purposes only. There is a further condition, namely that the income must:

> 'arise in respect of rents or receipts from an estate, interest or right vested in any person for charitable purposes.'

This appears to mean that the property must be held for charitable purposes and not, by implication, for investment or fundraising purposes.

The subsection appears on the face of it to exclude charities which are embodied as limited companies or unincorporated associations. In fact, the interpretation of this section is drawn more widely. If we take into account s 9(4) of ICTA 1988, which makes income tax exemptions available to bodies which pay corporation tax, as do companies and unincorporated associations, then the s 505 reliefs become available to all types of charitable organisation.

The legal definition of 'land' in the Interpretation Act 1978 states 'Land includes buildings and other structures, land covered with water, and any estate, interest, easement, servitude or right in or over land ...' The type of income taxed will be principally rent, but will include *feu* duties, lease premiums, and income from the letting of sporting rights. The relevant schedule is Schedule A.

Profits from the development of land are not covered by the exemption in s 505(1)(a). At first sight, such profits may appear to be capital items and, as such, outside the scope of income tax. Prior to the introduction of capital gains tax, such profits would have escaped tax altogether if it were not for two strategies of the tax authorities. First, such profits could be regarded as 'an adventure in the nature of trade' and therefore taxable as trading profits under Schedule D Case I;[1] or secondly, they could be caught by a specific piece of anti-avoidance legislation, now s 776 of ICTA 1988, where they would be deemed to be Schedule D Case VI income. If either strategy succeeded, these profits would in any event be exempt under s 505(1)(a); after all they appear to arise from land. However, this is not the case, because in respect of D I the source is trade not land; and in respect of s 776, because it is a special

---

[1]   See Chapter 4 for a discussion of trading by charities.

anti-avoidance measure, any exemption which may have been available is overridden.

Section 505(1)(b) and (1)(c)(i) are no longer of any relevance.

Section 505(1)(c)(ii) originates in the 1842 Act and refers to income arising under Schedule D Case III, which taxes interest, annual payments, discounts and public revenue income.

2.2.2   Interest

The exemption is applicable to 'yearly' or annual interest only, which would mean that interest on a loan repayable on demand, for example an overdraft, would not be exempt. This rather esoteric distinction between annual and non-annual interest is rendered obsolete by ESC B9, which effectively exempts all interest a charity is likely to receive (so long as applied solely to charitable purposes). Building society interest, which normally has tax deducted, will be paid gross if the charity fills in the relevant form, thus avoiding the need to make a claim. Bank interest paid to companies will be paid gross, and will be paid gross to charitable trusts on completion of the relevant form.

2.2.3   Annual payments

The position prior to the Finance Act 1990 was that in order for donations to charity to be tax-effective, they had to be treated as 'annual payments'. In general, these are settlements of income, meaning that a person has severed his ownership of part of his income, and settled it on someone else. This severance has to be recognised by law if there are to be any tax benefits. The severed income becomes part of the income of the person upon whom it has been settled. Annual payments are sometimes known as charges on income, which conveys the idea that they are a deduction from, or charge on, a person's total income.

Prior to 1 April 2000, the only tax-effective annual payments that remained for the individual were charitable annual payments. For annual payments to have beneficial tax consequences, the donor had to make a legally binding transfer of part of his income to the charity, which could not be revoked by the donor within the first three years. This was done by the donor entering into a charitable deed of covenant. The payments under the deed had to be 'annual', which meant a commitment to a payment each year. There were no minimum or maximum amounts. The scheme was founded on the presumption that the charity was legally entitled to the income and, if unpaid, could sue for it. There are, however, no known instances of this.

2.2.4   Gift Aid

The Finance Act 1990 introduced Gift Aid, which meant that one-off net donations of at least £250 would be treated as if they had been made under a deed, giving the same tax advantages to donor and charity. The Finance Act

2000 has extended Gift Aid, as we describe in Chapter 3, but the legal theory and tax effects remain the same as for the old annual payments. The machinery of tax collection for annual payments links charity and donor reliefs, and the nature of this machinery means that such payments are beneficial to both parties.[1]

Annual payments are taxable on the recipient under Schedule D Case III, but tax is deducted at basic rate by the payer so the recipient receives a net amount. Section 505(1)(c)(ii) exempts annual payments received by charities from income and corporation tax, so the recipient of an annual payment will be able to claim back any tax previously deducted. Thus, the charity will first receive a net amount, and then claim back basic rate tax (at present, 22/78ths of the donation) from the Revenue.

The payer of an annual payment in favour of a charity can deduct it from that part of his income which bears the highest rate of tax. Thus, a higher rate taxpayer can reduce the amount of higher rate tax he pays by making such a payment. Relief will be given at $(40\% - 22\%$ ie $18\%) \times$ grossed-up annual payment, and will be made by the Revenue adjusting the payer's PAYE coding.

The charity can reclaim tax deducted, and the payer receive higher rate relief, only if the donor pays an amount of income tax or CGT equal to the basic rate tax the charity will reclaim. If the donor pays less tax than this, the Revenue will make an assessment on the donor for any shortfall under s 350 of ICTA 1988.

A simple example of the process is as follows. Rex pays £780 to a charity and agrees with them that it should be treated as a Gift Aid donation. He is a higher rate tax payer. Rex pays a cheque for £780 to the charity. He is deemed to be paying this net of tax. The charity receives the £780 and can reclaim from the Revenue the tax Rex is deemed to have deducted, which is £780 × 22/78 = £220. The charity is better off by £1,000.

The cost of the donation for Rex is less than £780, because he can reduce his higher rate tax by the amount of the grossed-up payment, ie £1,000. He pays £1,000 × 18% = £180 less higher rate tax than he would have paid if he had not made the payment. The final cost to Rex of the donation is therefore £780 − £180 = £600.

The annual payments should be 'pure income profit' in the hands of the charity (the term is from case-law, not statute[2]). This means that the charity should not provide anything in return for the income. The settlement of the income should have been freely entered into without the prospect of a return on investment, apart from feelings of human kindness.

---

1   The machinery of tax deduction on annual payments and interest is contained in ICTA 1988, ss 348–350.

2   *IRC v National Book League* 37 TC 455.

One point to bear in mind, from the charity's point of view, is that the provision of benefits in exchange for funds may be construed as trading. What, after all, is trading other than the provision of goods or services in return for a contribution? Trading income is taxable for the charity unless it fulfils some strict requirements. Section 505(1)(c) does not exempt trading income, such exemptions are to be found in s 505(1)(e).

2.2.5 Other provisions

Prior to 1965, company profits were dealt with directly under the income tax system. Corporation tax was introduced in 1965 and this required the addition of Schedule F to deal with the taxation of company dividends and distributions. These dividends would be taxable on the charity if not for the exemption under s 505(1)(c)(iii).

The importance of the second paragraph in subsection (c) has already been mentioned. The wording is from the Income Tax Act 1803. There can be situations where a bona fide charity, whose income is applicable to charitable purposes only, does not actually so apply it but spends it, for instance, on private luxury accommodation for senior employees.

Section 505(1)(d) concerns income from government stock taxable under Schedule D Case III which is used in one particular way. This dates from the Income Tax Act 1842 and clearly predates the *Pemsel* judgment, where the advancement of religion was recognised as a charitable purpose, thus rendering the subsection unnecessary.

Section 505(1)(e) exempts charitable trading in certain situations and looks at first sight more generous than it actually is. The implications of its provisions are complex and warrant separate discussion, to be found in Chapter 4.

The rest of s 505 contains subsections introduced by the Finance Act 1986 and which are chiefly concerned with tax avoidance and its prevention. We can compare the approach of modern tax legislation to that of earlier periods by noting that s 505(2)–(8) plus s 506 is at least as long again as the sections which preceded it in the legislation.

Section 505(2) converts a gift from one charity to another, which would otherwise have been outside the scope of income tax, into a potentially taxable receipt by bringing it into Schedule D Case III as if it were an annual payment. For this receipt to be eligible for the exemption in s 505(1)(c), it must be applicable and applied for charitable purposes only, thus placing a control on its use. Thus, the effects of the *Helen Slater*[1] case were reversed.

We have noted that exemption of income from tax was always, from the beginning, subject to the rule that it should be applicable and applied for charitable purposes only. The single sanction available to the tax authorities

---

1   *IRC v Helen Slater Charitable Trust Ltd* [1981] STC 471, CA.

was to refuse exemption to the particular income not spent on charitable purposes. By the early 1980s, this was not felt to be a sufficiently strong sanction. To act as a deterrent, the total tax relief obtained on other charity income could be threatened if the scale of non-charitable expenditure was sufficient.

2.3   THE RESTRICTION SCHEME

Section 505(3)–(6), s 506 and Sch 20 initiates a scheme by which charities lose relief under s 505(1) or in respect of CGT if they spend their funds on non-charitable objects. The wording of the legislation is tortuous. As Tony Blair said during the committee stage

> 'The new provisions ... are hideously complex ... it starts with a virtual triple negative which makes it extremely difficult to decide what it attempts to achieve.'[1]

The scheme operates by the use of four concepts: relevant income and gains; qualifying expenditure; non-qualifying expenditure; and total expenditure.

2.3.1   Relevant income and gains

This comprises (a) income of the charity which is taxable, such as trading income outside the requirements of s 505(1)(e); (b) income which is eligible for relief under s 505(1), such as covenant income; (c) all chargeable gains, whether or not eligible for relief under s 256 of TCGA. Relevant income does not include receipts outside the scope of income tax, such as legacies, gifts and donations, but does include Gift Aid donations because these have entered the tax net, although exempted.

2.3.2   Qualifying expenditure

This means expenditure incurred in the period under review for charitable purposes only. Expenditure for which a commitment has been made[2] (even if not yet contracted for) and which has not yet been spent during the period under review can be treated as incurred in that period. Section 506 contains certain requirements tightening up the phrase 'for charitable purposes only'. If payments are made to bodies outside the UK, the charity has to take 'reasonable steps' to ensure that the payment is applied for charitable purposes; if it does not then the expenditure does not qualify. It is essential, therefore, that evidence of review should be retained in case of query by the Revenue. There was concern during the committee stage of the Bill that Revenue clearance would have to be sought before funds were spent overseas. The then Chief Secretary to the Treasury, John MacGregor, stated what the actual position would be:

---

1   Parliamentary Papers 1986, Standing Committee G, column 489.
2   See ICTA 1988, s 506(2).

'The requirement does not mean that charities making payments overseas will need to obtain advance clearance from the Inland Revenue ... The following is what the Revenue expect. Usually, it will look at overseas payments as part of the normal process of dealing with the charity's annual claim for relief. In many cases, it will be obvious without further inquiry that the payments qualify for relief. But, where appropriate, the Revenue may need to ask the charity for information about the activities and objectives of the overseas body, and about arrangements for earmarking the payment for a particular purpose or checking on what it has been used. For example, the Revenue might ask to see a copy of correspondence with the overseas body about payments.'[1]

2.3.3 Non-qualifying expenditure

This means, succintly, expenditure which is not qualifying expenditure. There is a grey area in the case of administration expenditure. If the level of expenditure is reasonable in terms of the size of the charity and in comparison with its peers, then the whole of its administration expenditure should be classed as qualifying. However, where it is clear that charity funds are being used for an unusually high level of personal benefit of the employees, it is possible that such expenditure will be questioned. There is an absence of reported cases in relation to this legislation, so hard and fast rules cannot be laid down. If the charity invests its funds in investments which are outside the ambit of Schedule 20, or makes a non-qualifying loan, then these will be non-qualifying expenditure. The schedule states which investments and loans are eligible to be qualifying expenditure. The summary in IR 75 states[2] that the following kinds of investment are acceptable, the general rule being that investments at arm's length on the open market will be automatically acceptable: bank and building society deposit accounts; gilts and local authority bonds, shares traded on recognised investment exchanges; interests in land, excluding mortgages; and common investment funds under the Charities Act. Loans will qualify if they are to another UK charity for charitable purposes only, or to a beneficiary of a charity in the course of carrying out the charity's purposes. Care needs to be taken with loans to trading subsidiaries (see Chapter 4).

2.3.4 Other terms

Total expenditure is the total of qualifying and non-qualifying expenditure incurred by a charity in the period under review.

Non-taxable income is income outside the scope of income tax such as legacies and donations.

---

1   Parliamentary Papers 1986, Standing Committee G, columns 495–6A.
2   IR 75 *Tax Reliefs for Charities* (June 1987), p 5.

2.3.5 Applying the restriction scheme

To make sense of the restriction scheme, it is easiest to follow a series of questions, where certain consequences follow after each one.

KEY

RI is relevant income and gains.

QEX is qualifying expenditure.

NONQEX is non-qualifying expenditure.

TEX is total expenditure.

NONTAX is non-taxable income.

The stages in calculating whether there is any restriction on tax exemption are as follows:

1. Is the charity's RI > £10,000?

   Yes – go to (2);

   No – no restriction, end of calculation.

2. Is RI > QEX?

   Yes – go to (3);

   No – no restriction in this period, go to (5).

3. Is there any NONQEX?

   Yes – go to (4);

   No – no restriction, end of calculation.

4. Tax relief for that period is restricted by the lower of NONQEX, or the excess of RI over QEX.

5. Is TEX > RI?

   Yes – go to (6);

   No – restriction of relief confined to that period.

6. Deduct NONTAX from the lower of (TEX > RI) or NONQEX. If the result is positive go to (7) as this is the amount to be attributed to earlier years.

7. The maximum restriction for each earlier period is the surplus of total income over total expenditure.

How is the restriction of tax relief achieved? The charity, within 30 days of being notified that its relief will be restricted, can choose which part(s) of its income will suffer. If the charity only had two types of income, rent of £20,000 and gross gift aid donations of £20,000; and the restriction from point (4) above was £2,000, then the charity could only reclaim £2,000 from FICO instead of the full

£4,400 (£20,000 × 22%). If more than £2,000 has been reclaimed already the surplus will have to be repaid to the Revenue.

Higher rate relief previously given to donors can be withdrawn on donations of more than £1,000 per donor. If, in the above example, £2,000 of the Gift Aid income came from one higher rate taxpayer, and the person had received higher rate relief of £360 on the payment (£2,000 × 18%), then this person will have his relief restricted. The actual method of restriction is unknown as there are currently no reported examples of the restriction being applied.

The complexity of this specific legislation, particularly as it relates to previous years, seems absurd, but the overall aim at least is clear: to ensure that charities spend their funds on charitable purposes. It is unfortunate that the abuse of charitable status in the 1970s made action of this sort necessary, thus making life more difficult for those charities which have never abused their status.

These, then, are the main mechanisms which affect the way in which charities receive relief from income and corporation tax. The result is that most charities do not pay income tax and, although the system is antiquated, it operates reasonably well. Trading, however, is one area which can still cause problems. We have, therefore, devoted a chapter to it.[1]

---

1   See Chapter 4.

Chapter 3

TAX-EFFICIENT GIVING TO CHARITIES AND RELIEFS FOR DONORS

'It is better to give than to receive'

Source unknown

3.1   INTRODUCTION

Depending on its type, a gift made to charity may qualify for tax relief or exemption which the donor can claim, and/or entitle the charity to claim a tax repayment. Use of the available tax exemptions can bring considerable benefit to the charity, both by increasing the value of gifts where tax repayments are claimed and by encouraging people to make gifts in cases where the donor benefits from the exemption.

There have been considerable changes to the way in which individuals and companies give to charities in recent years. This is particularly true since the Budget of 2000. The proposed *Getting Britain Giving* measures, announced by the Chancellor in his Pre-Budget Report on 9 November 1999, were further improved in the Budget Statement on 21 March 2000. All the measures came into effect in April 2000.[1]

The Inland Revenue publishes very useful leaflets on giving to charity, setting out how businesses and individuals can obtain tax relief. Following the 2000 Budget, the Inland Revenue published a guidance note for charities – *Getting Britain Giving.*[2]

3.2   DEEDS OF COVENANT

A deed of covenant is a legal document placing an obligation on the donor to make regular payments to a charity.[3] To be tax effective, it must have been capable of running for a period of more than three years and have been incapable of earlier termination. The deed had to be in the correct legal form and include the word 'deed'.

---

1   FA 2000, Pt III, ch II, ss 38–44.
2   21 March 2000, subsequently updated, extended and reissued in November 2000. This is available on the web at www.inlandrevenue.gov.uk, as 'Guidance Notes for Charities'.
3   ICTA 1988, s 347A(7).

3.2.1 Tax treatment

Payments under a deed of covenant were treated for tax purposes as made net of basic rate tax. The charity could recover the tax from the Inland Revenue, increasing the value of the gift. Individuals who are liable to tax at the higher rate (40%) could also receive higher rate tax relief on their payments. For example, a payment of £78 would allow the charity to claim £22 from the Inland Revenue and reduce the tax bill of the higher rate taxpayer by £18. Claims for repayment were made annually, or more often, by completing the official single sheet form R68 accompanied by a schedule or schedules of income included in the claim.

3.2.2 Budget 2000 – changes

Covenant payments falling due on or after 6 April 2000 are covered by the new Gift Aid measures as the tax relief for covenants has been withdrawn. However, where a covenanted payment which fell due before 6 April 2000 was made on or after that date, the new Gift Aid measures will not apply to the payment. Instead, the existing rules for deeds of covenant continue to apply to the payment.

In particular, the rule entitling a charity to reclaim tax at the basic rate in force when the covenanted payment fell due, rather than when it was made, continues to apply to the payment. This means that if a charity receives a covenanted payment after 6 April 2000 which had legally fallen due before that date, it will not be disadvantaged by the reduction in the basic rate from 23% to 22% that came into force with effect from 6 April 2000.

As a transitional measure, charities will not have to obtain a Gift Aid declaration in respect of payments made under deeds of covenant which are already in existence and still remain in force at 6 April 2000. Effectively, the deed of covenant will stand in place of the Gift Aid declaration. Charities should use the existing claim form R68 and schedules to reclaim tax for covenanted payments by individuals received on or after 6 April 2000 but which fell due before that date. However, any declarations made outside the terms of the deed or after the expiry of the deed must be covered by a Gift Aid declaration. Likewise, quite clearly a new deed of covenant introduced on or after 6 April 2000 must be covered by a Gift Aid declaration.

Charities should consider carefully before they assume that an existing covenant has no continuing benefit and either cancel it or decide not to make use of a covenant agreement in the future. In some cases, it will be very useful, or possibly essential, to retain existing covenants and for future arrangements with the donor to involve the legal structure which a covenant provides. As has been seen, from April 2000, a covenant will not be able on its own to produce the well-known tax benefits, but it is still a legal document. However, donations made in future under a covenant arrangement must also qualify as Gift Aid for the charity to reclaim basic rate tax.[1]

3.3   GIFT AID

The Finance Act 1990 introduced the concept of a new type of relief for single gifts by individuals made on or after 1 October 1990.

3.3.1   General rules prior to 5 April 2000

One-off donations are called Gift Aid. They are treated as net of tax and a tax repayment can be claimed in a similar way to donations under a covenant. On introduction, Gift Aid required a minimum donation of £600. This was progressively reduced to £400 with effect from 1 July 1992, and to £250 with effect from 16 March 1993 until 5 April 2000. The maximum limit of £5 million was removed in the 1991 Budget, although it is accepted that this has had little or no effect on giving.

The donor had to be a UK resident and the gift had to be made out of taxed income and could not be due under a deed of covenant or under a payroll deduction scheme. Any benefit received by the donor could not exceed 2.5% of any gift up to a maximum of £250 in any one year.

The gift had to be in cash with no conditions attached. Clearly, fundraising collections that were not a gift out of one individual's taxable income did not qualify, nor did the writing off of a loan to a charity or several small taxable gifts amounting to £250 in total; each gift had to be for at least £250 net of basic rate tax. Only outright gifts could qualify.

A donor who paid higher rate tax could claim further tax relief. Companies could also make gifts under Gift Aid and in this case there was no minimum except for close companies, as defined by ICTA 1988, s 414 where the minimum of £250 still applied.

3.3.2   Millennium Gift Aid

Millennium Gift Aid was a particular type of Gift Aid scheme introduced by the Chancellor in his March 1998 Budget. It was superseded by the 2000 Budget.[2]

3.3.3   Budget 2000 – changes

Considerable improvements were announced in the 2000 Budget. They are undoubtedly causing a change in the way in which individuals and companies give to charity. The changes include:

---

1   FA 2000, Pt III, ch II, s 41.
2   See further, FA 2000, Pt III, ch II, s 42.

- abolishing the £250 minimum limit for Gift Aid donations, which means that the scheme applies to any donation, whether large or small, regular or one-off;
- withdrawing the separate tax relief for payments made under a deed of covenant so that in future the relief for any payments is under the Gift Aid scheme;
- replacing the requirement for donors to give the charity a separate Gift Aid certificate for each donation with a requirement to give a new, simpler and more flexible Gift Aid declaration;
- allowing donors to make Gift Aid donations over the telephone or Internet without having to complete and sign a paper declaration;
- removing the requirement that donors must pay basic rate income tax equal to the tax deducted from their donations and simply requiring them to pay an amount of income tax or CGT, at any rate, equal to the tax deducted from their donation;
- allowing donors to claim higher rate tax relief for donations against either income tax or CGT;
- removing the requirement for companies, including companies owned by a charity, to deduct tax from their donations, which also means they will not need to complete a Gift Aid declaration form;
- allowing Crown servants and members of the UK Armed Forces serving overseas, other non-UK resident individuals who make donations out of income or gains charged to UK tax, and non-UK resident companies to make use of the Gift Aid scheme.

Historically, only donations by UK resident individuals and companies could qualify as Gift Aid donations. This last measure means that effectively from April 2000 the list of those who can make donations which will qualify is extended to include:

- individuals who are resident in the UK;
- individuals who are Crown servants or members of the UK Armed Forces serving overseas;
- other non-resident individuals, provided they have income or capital gains charged to UK tax that are at least equal to the gross amount of the donation (ie the donation before deduction of basic rate income tax); and
- companies, whether or not they are resident in the UK.

The new measures came into force for individual donations made on or after 6 April 2000 and company donations made on or after 1 April 2000.[1]

---

1   FA 2000, Pt III, ch II, ss 39 and 40.

3.3.4 Forms

Gift Aid declarations are the new forms which replace the old Gift Aid certificates. The final model version[1] of the new form is much simpler and more flexible to use than its predecessor.

The way in which the new system operates does appear to be more flexible. Donors will be able to provide a declaration in advance of their donation, at the time they make the donation or at any time after the donation, subject of course to the normal time-limit within which a charity can reclaim tax. The declaration will also be able to cover one donation or any number of donations and can be made in writing or orally.

The amount of information required by the Inland Revenue to be shown on a Gift Aid declaration has, in their words, 'been kept to the minimum consistent with proper administration of the tax relief'. There is also, of course, the need for charities to be able to show an adequate audit trail. It is perfectly feasible, if a charity so wishes, to add further information and notes of their own. However, in certain cases, it may be necessary to add further information to satisfy particular legal requirements. For example, when the information provided by the donor is to be used for purposes other than reclaiming tax, the Data Protection Act 1998 requires that this be explained to the donor.

Additionally, if the organisation is a registered charity and incorporates the Gift Aid declaration into its fundraising and appeals literature, the Charities Act 1993 requires that a statement is included in the fundraising and appeals literature which shows that the organisation is a registered charity. Charities will be able to design their own Gift Aid written declaration form but it must contain:

- the charity's name;
- the donor's name;
- the donor's address;
- a description of the donation(s) to which the declaration relates;
- a declaration that the donation(s) is/are to be treated as Gift Aid donation(s);
- a note explaining that the donor must pay an amount of income tax or CGT equal to the tax deducted from his donation(s).

As can quite clearly be seen from the above list, the Inland Revenue is not insisting that the declaration be dated and signed. Nevertheless, many charities will for their own peace of mind still seek to obtain the donor's signature. In the case of a written declaration, charities may pre-print as much of the information on the declaration form as they wish, for example the charity's name. There is no need to obtain approval from the Inland Revenue for a charity's own-designed declaration but in its Guidance Notes the Revenue

---

1   Published with *Getting Britain Giving* 21 March 2000.

makes it clear that FICO will be happy to approve a charity's written declaration form if the charity so desires.

The Finance Act 2000 now provides for gifts made orally. Where information is collected, for example over the telephone, the charity must confirm the donation in writing to the donor. This confirmation must include:

– all the details provided by the donor in his oral declaration;
– a note explaining that the donor must pay an amount of income tax or CGT equal to the tax deducted from his donation(s);
– a note explaining the donor's entitlement to cancel the declaration retrospectively;
– the date on which the donor gave the declaration; and
– the date on which the charity sent the written record to the donor.

In this case, a charity may give the information to the donor and ask him to confirm it, instead of asking the donor to provide the information verbally.

This procedure should be carried out in order to ensure that the charity can reclaim the tax in respect of the donation. All these records will need to be kept as part of an audit trail should there be a subsequent Inland Revenue audit.

Donors are entitled to cancel their declarations at any time. They can do this by notifying the charity in writing or orally. Obviously, charities should keep a record of the cancellation of a declaration, including the date of the donor's notification. Subject to this, cancellation of a declaration has effect only in relation to donations received by the charity on or after:

– the date on which the donor notifies the charity of the cancellation, or
– such later date as the donor may specify.

Charities must not reclaim tax in respect of donations for which the declaration has been cancelled. Any donations received before the date of the donor's notification will still qualify as Gift Aid donations. However, donations given under an oral declaration which is then cancelled within a period of 30 days after the charity has sent the donor the written record will be treated as non-qualifying. In other words, it would be as if the declaration had never been made.

Whilst charities do not have to wait for the 30-day period to expire on oral declarations before reclaiming tax in respect of donations, it would probably be sensible to do so. This is because where the tax is reclaimed by the charity within the 30-day period and the donor then subsequently cancels his declaration within that same period, the charity will have to refund to the Inland Revenue the tax which it has claimed. To make it even more complex, if this situation has arisen then, by negotiation with IR (Charities), it may be possible to deduct the over-claim from the next tax reclaim.

The charity's full name, usual name or acronym will suffice in completing the declaration form, provided that one is able to identify the charity adequately from that name. In order to establish an audit trail to the donor, charities are advised to obtain as full details of the donor's name and address as possible. Although the Guidance Notes require merely the donor's name and address, the charity may have to obtain further information to show that the tax reclaim is correct in the event that IR (Charities) carries out an audit of the tax reclaim and the information provided is insufficient to enable them to trace the donor. It therefore makes sense to obtain this information for each and every donor on the declaration form in the first place.

Ideally, the Guidance Notes suggest that charities should obtain the donor's full title, forenames and surname or, at the very least, the individual's initials and surname, as well as his full postal address, including the postcode. Where a donor, who continues to make donations, subsequently changes his name or address, this will not invalidate the declaration. However, charities must keep a record of the updated information whenever they are notified of a change in the donor's name or address.

The description of the donation to which a declaration relates can be whatever the charity wants. However, *Getting Britain Giving* Guidance Notes suggest that a charity should use one of the following phrases:

–   the donation of £x I made to you on dd/mm/yy;
–   the enclosed donation;
–   all donations I make under the direct debit mandate below;
–   all donations I make on or after the date of this declaration;
–   all donations I make from this date until further notice; or
–   all donations I have made since 6 April 2000 and all donations I make hereafter.

Whether one of these descriptions is chosen or the charity devises its own, it is very important that the description is correct. The declaration will not cover any donations received that fall outside the description used. It is particularly relevant where the description chooses a date that is later than that of a number of donations made by the donor to the charity. Depending on the description used, a declaration may apply to all future donations.

There is no requirement in the Finance Act 2000 for declarations to be renewed periodically. However, as a matter of good practice, it is sensible to remind donors from time to time that they have opted to treat their donations as Gift Aid donations. This is because individuals' circumstances change and they may no longer be paying sufficient income tax or CGT to cover the tax deducted from their donations. Where this occurs the donor may incur additional liability to tax and, from a fundraising point of view, it is essential that they are not faced with a tax bill from the Inland Revenue. Whenever a donor wishes to alter the description of his donations to a charity, he should cancel the original declaration and make a fresh one.

When it comes to the declaration that donations are to be treated as being made under Gift Aid, charities can again devise their own wording, for example, as the Guidance Notes from the Inland Revenue point out:

- please treat my donations as Gift Aid donations;
- I want my donations to be Gift Aid donations;
- please reclaim tax on my donations;
- I want the charity to reclaim tax on my donations;
- I want the charity to reclaim tax on my donations ... Yes/No; or
- tick here if you want us to reclaim tax on your donations ( ).

Clearly, since the main objective of the 2000 Budget was to increase tax-efficient giving to charity, it is advisable to keep the form as simple as possible, therefore the last of the above options may be the most appropriate.

Finally on the subject of the declaration form, the guidance explains that charities can devise their own wording in relation to the tax requirement note and give two possible examples:

- you must pay an amount of income tax or CGT equal to the tax we reclaim on your donations (currently 28p for every £1 you give); or
- remember to notify us if you no longer pay an amount of income tax or CGT equal to the tax we reclaim on your donations (currently 28p for every £1 you give).

This change in the tax rules is of considerable advantage provided it operates properly. In order for a charity to reclaim a refund of the tax deemed to have been deducted before the donation is made, the donor no longer needs to match the gross amount with income taxed at the basic rate. Historically, this rule caused potential problems for individuals on lower incomes, often the most generous in giving to charity, who entered into deeds of covenant. In theory, and often in practice, the excess of the basic rate tax deducted from the covenant over the basic rate tax suffered by the donor (if any) could have been reclaimed from the donor by the Inland Revenue, as it was in several cases.

As a result of these changes flowing from the 2000 Budget, Gift Aid is much more tax-efficient and convenient because one-off payments can be made, however small. Additionally, the tax deducted from the payment needs only to be covered by the total tax suffered on the donor's income. These changes should enable more people on lower incomes to make use of Gift Aid.

As an example, if Fred Fish give £40 to charity under Gift Aid, this represents a gross payment (currently – September 2000) of £51.28, less tax of £11.28. Prior to 6 April 2000, if this payment had been made under a deed of covenant (as it was too small to be made under Gift Aid), Fred would have needed at least £51 of income taxed at the basic rate or higher for the charity to have been able to recover tax.

Now Fred will need to have suffered tax of only £11.28, which could simply come from £112.80 taxed at the 10% starting rate. This effectively means that charities should be able, in their fundraising, to approach individuals on low incomes who previously were unable to give tax-effectively under Gift Aid.

A charity may collect cash donations using envelopes, such as those used by churches or house-to-house street collectors. In these cases, where it is a one-off donation, the charity may pre-print the Gift Aid declaration on the envelope for completion by the donor and, provided this is completed correctly, the donation will then qualify under the Gift Aid scheme. Where the donor is already a regular supporter and the charity holds his Gift Aid declaration on file, the envelope need simply show either the donor's name or some other unique identification, such as a reference number which can be cross-referenced to the donor register. In practice, where envelopes containing the same unique identifier are used by the donor and his spouse and minor children, the charity can safely assume that all donations are from the donor. The charity should ensure that when the envelope is opened and the contents are counted, an official of the charity records the sum that it contained both on the envelope itself and in a donor record. This is to maintain the audit trail to which we will return later.

3.3.5 Benefits

Charities often provide their donors with a gift in an attempt to thank them. As the Inland Revenue puts it, provided these gifts are 'modest' the donation will still qualify as a Gift Aid donation. The Guidance Notes introduced certain limits that the value of the gift should not exceed. Where a charity wants to provide benefits to donors, for example, as part of a membership scheme, it will need to consider whether the benefits it intends to provide fall within these limits. Where the value of the benefit exceeds the limits, the gift cannot, of course, qualify as a Gift Aid donation.

Charities therefore need to determine on receipt of a Gift Aid donation whether the donor, or anyone connected with the donor, is receiving any benefit in consequence of making that donation and, if so, whether the value of the benefit exceeds the limits in the donor benefit rules.

(1) What is a benefit?
Effectively, there is no change from the old Gift Aid scheme and a mere acknowledgement of a donor's generosity in the charity's literature or by means of a plaque will not amount to a benefit, provided that the acknowledgement does not take the form of an advertisement for the donor's business.

A benefit is defined in the *Getting Britain Giving* Guidance Notes as 'any item or service provided by the charity or a third party to the donor or a person connected with the donor as a result of making the donation'; a very wide definition indeed.

(2) Valuing donor benefits
The method of valuing benefits, like the definition of what is a benefit, is unchanged from the previous Gift Aid scheme. However, as then, the valuation

of donor benefits can be extremely difficult. Where the benefit received by the donor or something comparable to it is also sold to the general public, whether by the charity or a third party, it is deemed that the value of the benefit received by the donor is the sale price to the public. In other words, where a donor receives a magazine that is available on the news stand, the value to the donor will be the cover price of the magazine. However, where it is not possible to do this and the benefit is less immediately obvious, charities must determine what a non-donor would be prepared to pay for the benefit.

Literature provided to donors, such as newsletters, annual reports, members handbooks, etc, which are not normally sold to the public and are published purely for the purpose of describing the work of the charity, will be deemed to have no value for the purposes of the donor benefit rules (detailed later in this Chapter). The right to attend the annual general meeting is also deemed to have no value.

A particular problem arises in respect of items purchased at a charity auction where the purchaser wants the payment to be treated as a Gift Aid donation. Bidding at charity auctions often means that the sale price is far in excess of the value of the item acquired. The Inland Revenue recognises that individuals purchasing items at a charity auction will very often intentionally pay more than they are worth in order to support the charity. Where a charity can show that the market value of an item purchased at a charity auction is less than the sale price, the charity can use the lower figure as the value of the item. Provided then that the two figures, ie the amount paid for the item and its true value, fall within the donor benefit rules, the Inland Revenue will allow the payment by the donor to qualify as a Gift Aid donation.

(3)   A special case – certain subscriptions
The pre-existing rule disregarding the benefit of right of admission to the premises of a heritage or wild life conservation charity, applicable only to the deed of covenant scheme, has been extended to the revised Gift Aid scheme. This relaxation covers only the donor or any member of his family and does not include non-family guests of the donor or any benefit other than the admission price.

The Inland Revenue has said that it recognises that, in practice, charities:

–   will often want to lay down rules for the maximum number of people that a donor may bring into the charity's premises; and
–   cannot be expected to check the identity and family relationship of people who seek admission to their premises.

Thus, for these purposes, any member of his family is very loosely defined as up to two other adults and six children. The Inland Revenue has confirmed that this can be applied not only to membership fees, but also to single admission charges. This is provided that the individual gives full details of name, address and how much is paid and states a wish for the tax relief to be claimed, thus meeting the Gift Aid rules. This means that an eligible charity could get an additional £2.80 on every £10 admission ticket.

3.3.6   Donor benefit rules

The rules relating to the benefits that a donor can receive from a charity following a gift to it have been amended to combine the old differing rules for covenants and Gift Aid, producing a very complex set of new rules. There are now two tests for the value of the benefits that a donor or person connected with the donor may receive.[1]

(1) The value of the benefits exceeds the limits in the table below (the 'relevant value' test):

Amount of donation	Value of benefits
£0–100	25% of total donations
£101–1,000	£25
£1,001+	2.5% of total donations

(2) The value of the benefits plus the value of any benefits received in consequence of any Gift Aid donations made by the same donor to the same charity earlier in the same tax year exceeds £250 (the 'aggregate value' test).

If the value of the benefits received exceeds either of these tests, the donation will not qualify as a Gift Aid donation.

(1)   Special 'relevant value' test benefit rule

The limits given in the table in the previous section (the 'relevant value' test) apply separately to each and every donation. However the Inland Revenue has introduced special rules which will apply to 'annualise' the amount of certain donations and the value of certain benefits for the purposes of applying the limits. Broadly, in the case of subscriptions under a membership scheme, these limits will normally apply by reference to the amount of the annual membership subscription and the value of the annual membership benefits. In other words, one compares the benefit that a donor receives with the annual subscription paid.

In this way, a charity can calculate whether the benefits in its membership scheme exceed the limit simply by looking at the annual membership subscription and the annual membership benefits. The result will be exactly the same whether the donor pays the membership subscription in one annual payment or by instalments throughout the year.

However, annualising will apply where a benefit (as the Inland Revenue puts it):

---

1   FA 2000, Pt III, ch II, s 39(5) and (6).

- consists of the right to receive benefits at intervals over a period of less than 12 months;
- relates to a period of less than 12 months;
- is one of a series of benefits received periodically in consequence of making a series of donations at intervals of less than 12 months; or
- is a one-off benefit received in consequence of making a donation which is one of a series of donations made at intervals of less than 12 months.

The operation of these rules is complex. The Inland Revenue is suggesting that in each of the first three categories, shown above, both the amount of the donation and the value of the benefit are annualised and then compared with the limits in the 'relevant value' test table. However, in the fourth category the amount of the donation, but not the value of the benefit, is annualised because the benefit is a one-off, and in that instance, the annualised donation and the value of the benefit will be compared with the limits in the 'relevant value' test table.

The Revenue is trying to achieve a consistency across all donations and related benefits and its Guidance Notes explain how the annualising should be carried out. It is fairly simple arithmetic. As noted, the first three categories relate benefits to 'a period' and the annualising is done on this basis as follows:

> 'multiplying the amount of the donation and where relevant the value of the benefit by 365, and dividing the result by
> - the number of days in the period of less than twelve months, or
> - the average number of days in the intervals of less than twelve months.'

This means that, in practice, where the period or the intervals are measured in calendar months, annualising can be done by reference to calendar months rather than days.

(2) Examples of 'relevant value' test benefit rule
The Inland Revenue Guidance Notes give examples, in respect of each of the categories set out above, of annualising benefits and donations to show whether or not the donation can qualify as a Gift Aid donation.

Let us take the case of a donor who makes monthly payments of £20 to a charity and as a result receives a monthly magazine that has a cover price of £2.50. The right to receive the magazine falls into the third category and therefore annualising needs to take place. Effectively, the annual amount of the donation is £240 and the annual value of the benefit is £30. As the annual value of the benefit exceeds the limit of £25 (ie the limit for donations of £101–£1,000) the donation therefore fails the 'relevant value' test and will not qualify as a Gift Aid donation.

In another example, a donor agrees to make monthly payments of £2 to charity for which he receives a one-off benefit worth £5. This falls into the fourth category listed in the previous section and therefore again, annualising will have to take place, but only to the donation as the benefit is a one-off. The annual value of the donation is £24 and the actual value of the benefit is £5. In this case, the value of the gift must not exceed 25% of the donation which would be £6 and, as it does not, the donation can qualify as a Gift Aid donation.

Finally, if we take the case of an individual making a single payment to a charity of £240 who, as a result, receives the right for a year to a monthly magazine which has a cover price of £2.50. In this case, the benefit related to the single payment of £240 is £30. The right to receive this benefit does not fall into any of the categories listed in the previous section so there is no need to annualise the benefit or the donation. Since the value of the benefit, £30, exceeds the limit of £25 (ie the limit for donations for £101–£1,000) the donation will fail the 'relevant value' test and will not qualify as a Gift Aid.

(3)   Special 'aggregate value' test benefit rule
The 'aggregate value' test is exactly the same as it was for the previous Gift Aid scheme. In particular, there is no need to annualise the value of benefits for the purposes of the 'aggregate value' test. Put simply, it is the actual value as opposed to the annual value of the benefits that count.

It is worth noting that, in addition to satisfying the 'relevant value' test, the value of benefits received in consequence of a donation must also satisfy the 'aggregate value' test if the donation is to qualify as a Gift Aid donation.

3.3.7   Split payments

Where the value of benefits would exceed the limits in the donor benefit rules, then the donor may specify that part of his gift is to be treated as a payment for the benefits and part is to be treated as a donation. Provided the donor specifies this before or at the time of making the donation, that part of the payment specified as a donation will qualify as a Gift Aid donation, provided it satisfies all the conditions for the tax relief.

3.3.8   Record-keeping

Charities will need to keep records to show that their tax reclaims are accurate. In other words, there must be an audit trail linking each donation to an identifiable donor who has given a valid Gift Aid declaration and all the other conditions for recovering tax must have been satisfied. These records do not have to be kept on paper and may be held on the hard drive of a computer, floppy disk, CD-Rom or stored on microfiche. However, where declarations are signed, they should always be kept in a form which preserves the signature, eg microfilm or electronically scanned in.

The form of records to be kept is not prescribed in any detail and does not appear to have changed significantly as a result of these new Gift Aid measures. Therefore, what this means in practice will depend on the size of the charity, the number of donations it has and the kind of systems in use.

The suggested length of time for keeping records for a charitable trust is somewhat confusing. To quote from Inland Revenue Guidance Notes for Charities (November 2000) at section 7.3.1, records must be kept until:

> 'the 31 January next but one after the end of the tax year to which your tax reclaim relates (for example, if you make a tax reclaim for the tax year 2000/2001, until 31 January 2003), or

> one year after you make your tax reclaim, rounded to the end of the next quarter (for example, if you make a tax reclaim on 25 May 2002, until 30 June 2003), or IR (Charities) completes any audit it has commenced which ever is the later.'

If the charity is a company, records have to be kept for six years after the end of the accounting period to which the tax claim relates. Effectively this sets out the minimum periods for which records must be kept by a charity. As IR (Charities) might carry out an audit of the tax reclaim at any time and discover errors which would then enable them to go back into earlier years, for at least six years, it may be in the best interests of the charity to keep records for longer than the minimum period set out above.

It is also worth remembering that if a donor has given the charity a declaration covering donations that he may make in the future, the charity will in any event need to keep the records relating to those declarations to enable it to reclaim tax on any future donations.

Where records are inadequate the charity may be required to repay the Inland Revenue any tax that it has reclaimed. In addition, there will be interest to pay on the tax and the charity may also be liable to a penalty. Effectively, this is no change from the pre-2000 Budget situation.

3.3.9   Audit

In the event that the Inland Revenue carries out an audit of a charity's tax reclaim, the auditor will usually ask to see the following information:

- any written Gift Aid declarations;
- in the case of oral Gift Aid declarations, a copy of the written records sent to the donor;
- any correspondence to or from the donors which relates to their Gift Aid donations;
- cash book recording receipt of cash donations;
- bank statements;
- credit card companies' statements; and
- any other records kept relating to donations, eg envelopes.

The Inland Revenue has published a Code of Practice (number 5) entitled *Inspection of Charities' Records*. This document sets out how IR (Charities) will carry out their audit inspections; in particular, it explains the charity's rights, promises that they will be treated fairly and courteously and sets out the help that IR (Charities) will provide where this is appropriate. A copy of the Code should be sent to any charity before an audit inspection is carried out by IR (Charities).

3.3.10   Reclaims

Reclaims of tax on donations post-April 2000 may be made on a new, simpler claim form with accompanying schedules. Charities no longer have to complete separate schedules for Gift Aid donations and covenanted payments, as there is only one type of schedule for all donations. Charities must enter the following details on this schedule for each donor:

–   the donor's name;
–   the date of the donation, or, where the claims cover more than one donation by the donor, the date of the last donation; and
–   the total amount of donations by the donor on which tax recovery is being claimed.

However, charities have to complete a separate schedule for each tax year, or part of the tax year, included in the claim. It is no longer necessary to calculate the tax relating to each donation separately. Charities are simply able to calculate the total tax reclaimed for all the donations shown on each schedule. Just before the budget, in March 2000, the Inland Revenue issued a letter to charities which gave details of:

–   new automated repayment services using BACS; and
–   the authorised signatory form.

Attached to the letter was a form, which had to be completed and returned to the Inland Revenue with the first repayment claim made on or after 6 April 2000. After that date, the Inland Revenue will repay only claims signed by an official of the charity who has been authorised on the form.

3.3.11   Additional points

Various computer aids are being developed to assist charities in calculating by how much the tax will increase a Gift Aid donation. Similar products will show higher rate tax payers how, by claiming back tax relief personally, they can make a higher donation to a charity and still only pay the amount they originally proposed to donate. One such set of web-enabled forms, written in Javascript, is being provided free for charities to download and incorporate onto their own website. The web link is http://www. itforcharities.co.uk/giftaid.htm.

Where an individual wants to give a valuable asset to charity a good fundraising strategy is to get the individual to sell the item and Gift Aid the proceeds. Because of the tax effect under Gift Aid, the charity thus receives more than it would have received if it had taken the asset and sold it. However, it is necessary to consider very carefully the capital gains and income tax position of the individual concerned and ensure that all the other usual conditions are met.

In England, Wales and Northern Ireland, a partnership of individuals does not have its own separate legal personality. So, effectively, a donation made by such a partnership is regarded by the Inland Revenue as having been made by the individual partners. By special exemption one partner may make a Gift Aid declaration on behalf of all the partners, provided that he has the power to do so under the terms of the partnership agreement. In this case, it would be sufficient for the declaration to show the name and address of the partnership rather than the names and addresses of all the individual partners. This means that a charity can obtain a tax-efficient Gift Aid declaration from a partnership without the requirement for each and every partner to make their own Gift Aid declaration. However, in Scotland a partnership does have a legal personality. Therefore, there is no need for an Inland Revenue exemption and in all cases one of the partners may make a Gift Aid declaration on behalf of the partnership showing the name and address of the partnership.

It is possible to combine the IHT exemption and Gift Aid. The donor's will should make a gift of money to a trusted individual and express a wish that the money should be given to charity. Where that individual makes the gift to charity within two years after the testator's death, IHT exemption is given to the estate and the charity can claim repayment of tax under the Gift Aid scheme. A gift made this way gives rise to tax reliefs of up to 93% of the amount of the gift. This scheme may be challenged by the Inland Revenue in the courts.

3.4   PAYROLL GIVING

With the agreement of the employer, it has always been possible for an employee to arrange for the employer to make donations from after-tax pay to a chosen charity.

The Finance Act 1986 introduced a scheme whereby, again with the agreement of the employer, an employee could have deductions made from pre-tax pay, and passed over to an 'agency' charity which in its turn would pass on the money to a charity or charities nominated by the employee. Employers who wish to set up such a scheme must make the necessary contractual arrangements with an agency charity approved by the Inland Revenue such as the Charities Aid Foundation. This scheme is known as give as you earn (GAYE).

3.4.1 Limits

The table below shows the maximum amount per year and per month (in brackets) which an individual has been able to give since payroll giving was introduced up until the last changes were announced.

Year	Per Annum	Per Month
1987	£120	(£10)
1988	£240	(£20)

1989	£480	(£40)
1990	£600	(£50)
1993	£900	(£75)
1996	£1,200	(£100)

There is no minimum sum.

3.4.2 Relief

A charity cannot claim any tax repayment on donations under a payroll giving scheme. The employee receives tax relief instead via the PAYE system. Thus, the cost to an individual of making the maximum gift of £1,200 per year in this way in 1999/2000 was £924 for the basic rate taxpayer and £720 for the higher rate taxpayer. In both cases, the charity received £1,200.

3.4.3 Budget 2000 changes

As part of the Government's campaign *Getting Britain Giving* there is a 10% supplement on all donations made under the Payroll Giving scheme during the period 6 April 2000–5 April 2003. This supplement is being made by the Government and is distributed to charities via the agencies currently running the scheme, and those agencies will do so without any deduction for administration fees.[1]

The Charitable Deductions (Approved Schemes) (Amendment) Regulations 2000[2] came into force on 6 April 2000. Agencies which distribute payroll giving donations to charities will have to distribute them to the chosen charity within 60 days. If an agency fails to distribute the donations within the time-limit, it will have to inform the Inland Revenue accordingly and explain why it has not done so.

Some payroll giving agencies have issued vouchers to employees in respect of their donations; the employees can then give these vouchers to the charities of their choice to redeem from the agency. As this practice is continuing to simplify the administration of the 10% supplement, agencies will add the supplement to the employee's donation account in which case the amounts shown on the vouchers given to the charities will include the supplement.

Additionally, with effect from 6 April 2000, the £1,200 per year maximum limit on the amount that an employee can give under this scheme was abolished. In future, there will be no limit.

3.4.4 Marketing

Using payroll giving by arranging for a group of employees to join together and give can engender a great sense of belonging. Marketing is important and visits

---

1   FA 2000, Pt III, ch II, s 38.
2   SI 2000/759.

by personnel from the charity concerned to address employees are important in promoting these schemes and keeping them operational. As the charity will need to involve the company before payroll giving can take place, another way of increasing the charity's income would be to persuade the company to make a payment under Gift Aid, matching that of its employees.

3.5   CORPORATE GIVING

So far, this chapter has looked primarily at gifts to a charity from an individual's viewpoint. The following sections examine company giving. Businesses, whether they are in the form of limited companies, partnerships or self-employed individuals, can help charities in several ways.

3.5.1   Deeds of covenant and Gift Aid

Prior to 1 April 2000, limited companies could make donations by deed of covenant or Gift Aid in the same way as individuals. The charity's right to claim tax repayment was the same as for individuals, except that different forms were used, but the company's tax position was different. The company had to make the payment to the charity net of basic rate tax in the same way as an individual, but had to pay the basic rate tax to the Inland Revenue, or set it off against the basic rate tax deducted on any payments that it received net of tax (such as interest received, other than from a bank).

The company received tax relief for the net payments plus relief against its corporation tax. This meant that, for a company paying corporation tax at the small companies' rate (20%), a covenanted or Gift Aid payment to charity resulted in the charity receiving, for example, a total of £100 at a cost to the company of £80. For a company paying corporation tax at the full rate (30%), the cost to the company of £100 received by the charity was £70.

This has now changed following the 2000 Budget. Gifts to charities by companies are now made gross and the company will receive tax relief on the full amount of its donation. Companies, including those owned by charities, will now no longer have to deduct tax from their Gift Aid donations or provide a Gift Aid declaration form. Therefore, charities should not reclaim tax on any donations they receive from a company. However, if a company incorrectly deducts tax from its donation, the charity will have to advise the company about the new rule accordingly and ask it to pay over the sum it has incorrectly deducted.

This applies to all Gift Aid donations by a company made on or after 1 April 2000 including covenanted payments, even if under a deed of covenant executed before that date. As an example, suppose that a deed of covenant written on 1 April 1999 provided for a company to make covenanted payments to a charity of £1,000 net of tax per annum. This is the amount that the company would have paid in the tax year to 31 March 2000. The charity would have recovered tax at the basic rate then existing (23%), thus reclaiming £298.70 from the Inland Revenue, making effectively a gross donation of just under £1,300. In order to maintain this level of donation after 1 April 2000, the charity would have to ask the company to make a payment to it of the gross amount, ie £1,298.70, and advise the company that it needs to claim the tax relief when calculating its profits for corporation tax.

3.5.2   Gifts of services and in kind

A business can help a charity by providing the services of an employee free or at a reduced rate. A special tax relief allows the salary and other costs of such an employee to be a tax-deductible trading expense of the business, even though the employee is not working for the business.[1] The secondment should be on a basis that is expressed as, and intended to be of, a temporary nature. 'Temporary' is not precisely defined, but most secondments to charity (which are rarely for more than two years and often for a year or less) would qualify. There is no VAT charge on the value of the employee's services.

If a company makes a gift of stock or equipment to a charity there are various ways in which this can be handled, each with different tax implications. Gifts to charity are allowable for tax purposes where made wholly and exclusively for the purposes of the trade of the company or where they can be justified as so being made.[2] Small gifts to local bodies which are not charities are similarly allowable under extra-statutory concession (ESC B7).

When calculating taxable profits, the business may deduct the cost of the gift as long as the cost would have been deductible if the item had not been donated, but instead had been used by the company in its normal business. Therefore, the cost of a computer donated to a charity would not have been allowable under this concession because it is a capital item. This rather restricted the value of the concession because capital items are more likely to be of use to a charity than revenue items. ESC B7 specifies that for gifts to be allowable they must also be:

> '... made for the benefit of a body or association of persons established for educational, cultural, religious, recreational or benevolent purposes, and the body is first local in relation to the donor's business activities, and second not restricted to persons connected with the donor.'

In addition, the expenditure on the gift should be 'reasonably small' in relation to the scale of the donor's business. No hard and fast rules were laid down as to how this was to be defined.

Some changes were made with effect from 27 July 1999 so that relief is available to companies (including individuals) carrying on a trade who give certain articles to charities. The gift must consist of either:

---

1   ICTA 1988, s 86.
2   ICTA 1988, s 577(9).

–   articles manufactured, or of a type sold, in the course of the donor's trade;
    or
–   machinery or plant used in the donor's trade.

Where the donor is eligible for relief, no amount is required to be brought into account for tax purposes in respect of the donated article, either as a trading receipt or, for capital allowance purposes, as a disposable value. However, if the donor receives any benefit attributable in any way to the gift, the donor is taxable on an amount equal to the value of the benefit.[1]

3.5.3   Sponsorship

A common means by which businesses help charities is by sponsoring the charity or, more usually, one of its events. This can take several forms, including payment of a fixed sum of money, the provision of facilities or goods, or the payment of a percentage of sales of certain goods sold by the company.

There are no special tax reliefs to allow a business to claim a tax deduction for the amount it spends on sponsorship. However, under the general tax rules for business expenses, the business can claim a tax deduction if the money was spent 'wholly and exclusively' for the purpose of trade. Where sponsorship involves a measure of publicity for the sponsor, as is usual, this condition should be met, as the sponsorship will, in effect, form part of the business's advertising and promotion budget.

Where a business receives such consideration for its sponsorship payments, the payments are not pure gifts and may be regarded as trading income of the charity. The charity may be liable to VAT on the sponsorship payment if the sponsor receives publicity or other facilities in return.[2]

Payments received from affinity credit cards are regarded as trading income, although by special exemption only 20% of the income is treated as VAT-able.[3] This concession, negotiated by the CTRG, means that the income from such credit cards is split into income relating to payment for services supplied by the charity and a donation or annual payment for which the charity provides no consideration.

HM Customs and Excise guidance is that only 20% of the initial payment is standard-rated income, the rest being a donation and outside the scope of VAT. The Inland Revenue advises that if, instead of a single contract between the charity and the donor, the contract is split between the charity and its trading subsidiary, it is possible for the part received by the charity to be exempt from tax as an annual payment.

---

1   FA 1999, s 55.
2   See further, Chapter 10.
3   See VAT Notice 701/1/95, p 15.

3.5.4 Other gifts by businesses

Other gifts to charity are tax-deductible by Inland Revenue concession (ESC B7), provided that:

– the gift is reasonably small in relation to the donor's business activities;
– the charity is local to the business;
– the charity is not only for the benefit of people connected with the business;
– the gift is 'wholly and exclusively' for the purpose of the trade (which means broadly that the business must gain some benefit from the gift).

The business is liable to VAT on the value of goods it gives to charity unless the goods cost £15 or less or are of a type that are zero-rated or exempt. However, if it makes a small charge for the goods, the business will pay VAT only on the amount that it charges.

3.5.5 Loans by businesses

This is yet a further example of anti-avoidance legislation being relaxed by concession in favour of donors to charities. Under existing Inland Revenue practice, it is understood that an interest-free loan to a charity does not result in adverse tax consequences for the lender. The requirements that must be met are:

– the loan is in cash;
– there is no arrangement as to its application, ie it must be for the general purposes of the charity and cannot be restricted to a specific purpose;
– the loan will be repaid in cash;
– the loan is not part of a larger arrangement.

Since the relief is concessionary, charities are advised to establish the Inland Revenue's approval of the arrangements in advance, especially where large sums are involved.[1]

3.5.6 Results of Budget 2000 changes

Problems very quickly emerged as a result of the change making company giving gross of tax, because many companies continued to write cheques to charities for the same amount as they had previously given, particularly where this was under a deed of covenant. This occurred because they failed to appreciate that, as their donations were now gross, the charity had been deprived of the vital tax reclaim. As we have seen, under the old system companies would make a donation, submit a Gift Aid form and allow the charity to claim back basic rate tax. The company separately paid the tax to the Inland Revenue, which was deducted from its gross taxable profits. Donations are now paid gross, but many companies appear to be unaware of the change and

---

1   FA 2000, Pt III, ch II, s 45.

charities are having to spend considerable time and effort to ensure that the donations they are receiving are as effective and efficient as they were prior to the change.

3.5.7 Donor reliefs

Two further significant aids to charitable giving were announced in the 2000 Budget. These primarily provided the tax relief to the donor.

(1) Gifts of shares

Tax relief will be granted to the donor where listed shares and securities, units in authorised unit trusts, shares in open-ended investment companies, holdings in foreign collective investment schemes and unlisted shares and securities dealt in on a recognised stock exchange (such as shares traded on the Alternative Investment Market), are given or sold at an under-value to a charity. This is in addition to the existing relief (when calculating capital gains) for gifts of shares, securities and other assets to charity, and will be set off as a deduction against the individual or company's income or profit for tax purposes. This new relief came into effect from 1 April 2000 for companies, and 6 April 2000, for individuals.[1]

Donors will be able to claim this deduction in the tax year in which the disposal takes place. The amount deductible will be the market value of the shares or securities on the date of disposal, plus any incidental costs of disposing of the shares, less any consideration given in return for disposing of the shares and the value of any other benefits received by the donor as a consequence of disposing of the shares.

Charities will not be in a position to reclaim any tax on donations of shares which they receive, as the donors can claim the tax relief at their top rate of tax on their self-assessment or corporation tax return.

(2) Gifts of certain trusts

A relaxation of the income tax provisions affecting people who settle property on UK-resident trusts and remain beneficiaries was introduced where the beneficiaries also include a charity. The income on which the settlor of a settlor-interested trust is chargeable to tax under Part XV of ICTA 1988 will be reduced by an amount equal to the income that is paid by the trust to the charity.[2]

These provisions broadly ensure that settlor-interested in-possession trusts and settlor-interested trusts are taken outside the provisions of the tax Acts to the extent that income arising to the trustees in the year is given to a charity. The provisions do not apply to bare trusts – that is, trusts in which the beneficiaries have an indefeasibly vested interest in the capital and income of the trust – and,

---

1   FA 2000, Pt III, ch II, s 43.
2   FA 2000, Pt III, ch II, s 44.

in such a case, any payment by the trustees to a charity would be treated as a payment by the beneficiary and would potentially qualify under the Gift Aid provisions.

Settlors affected by these changes will no longer need to include on their self assessment returns income which the new provisions take outside the charge to tax. A revised version of the self-assessment helpsheet is available which explains the changes and helps settlors calculate the amounts of taxable income.

3.6   HIGHER RATE TAXPAYERS

Individuals who pay tax on any part of their income at 40% are 'higher rate tax payers'. The number of individuals falling into this tax bracket has increased exponentially over the last few years and the 2000 Budget now allows these individuals to claim relief against either income tax or CGT for their donations to charities.

Three illustrations follow of how this works in relation to Gift Aid, payroll giving and gifts of shares, which show that from the individual's point of view the most tax-efficient is gifting shares. This is because the multiplier effect, which is found by dividing the amount received by the charity by the cost to the donor, is highest (3.57) for gifts of shares.

In the first example, using Gift Aid, if a donor gives £10,000 net (78%) then the Inland Revenue will refund to the charity the basic rate tax which would have been suffered on the donation, ie £2,821 (£10,000 × 22/78). Thus, the value of the gift to the charity is £12,821. Where the donor is a higher rate taxpayer and has suffered tax at 40% then he can reclaim from the Inland Revenue 18% of the gross amount, which is £2,308; 18% being the difference between the basic rate of 22% and the higher rate of 40%. As the donor has given a cheque for £10,000 to the charity and received £2,308 from the Inland Revenue, this reduces the cost to the donor to £7,692 (£10,000 − £2,308) and means that the multiplier effect is 1.67 (£12,821 ÷ £7,692).

Turning now to a similar example under payroll giving, using somewhat smaller numbers, where a donor agrees to give out £200 of his monthly pay, ie £2,400 per annum. This is the gross amount, which under payroll giving, will cost a higher rate taxpayer £1,440 per annum (£2,400 − 40% of £2,400). During the three-year period to 31 March 2003, as there is a 10% Government bonus in place, the charity will receive £2,640 from the payroll giving agency, less the usual administration charge. The multiplier effect will be a maximum, assuming no administration charge, of 1.83 (£2,640 ÷ £1,440).

Finally, turning to a gift of shares from a higher rate taxpayer worth £10,000, which cost £2,000 and which the charity sells for the market value of £10,000. The donor will receive income tax relief at 'full value' equal to £4,000 (40% of

£10,000) and CGT relief of £3,200 (40% of £10,000 − £2,000). Therefore, the net cost to the donor is £2,800 giving a multiplier effect of 3.57.

Chapter 4

TRADING BY CHARITIES

'To trade or not to trade that is the question?'

Anonymous Charity Finance Director

4.1 INTRODUCTION

By ICTA 1988, the trading income of charities is not normally exempt from tax unless it falls into one of two narrow categories. Most fundraising activities are exempt provided that they meet certain conditions. Any other trading activities in which a charity wants to engage should normally be carried on by a separate company owned by the charity. Provided that the funds of the charity are invested in such a company in accordance with Charity Commission guidelines and those of the Inland Revenue, the charity's tax exemptions should not be restricted.

The Inland Revenue published (in April 1995) a very useful booklet in its Charities Series CS2 entitled *Trading by Charities.* This offers some extremely good guidelines on the tax treatment of trades carried on by charities and should be read thoroughly by any charity considering trading. This booklet is currently being updated and revised following the 2000 Budget.

A charity is liable to tax on trading profits which fall outside the exempt categories. One example of this, historically, has been underwriting commission where a charity has underwritten a new issue of shares and for the risk of so doing has received a small commission without necessarily buying any of the shares. The commission received, less appropriate expenses, ie the profit, is liable to tax. The Inland Revenue effectively regards any profits derived from underwriting carried out by a charity as taxable. This is because either they are deemed to fall within Schedule D Case I as trading income, ie where it is done on a regular basis, or, where it is not trading income, the profits are chargeable under Schedule D Case VI.

4.2 FUNDRAISING ACTIVITIES

It is clear that many of the traditional and now generally accepted ways of charity fundraising could be classed as trading. The Inland Revenue has recognised that considerable problems could result if it attempted to enforce tax conditions on certain activities.

Therefore, the profit generated from fundraising activities, such as jumble sales, bazaars, carnivals, fireworks displays and similar events, although they are strictly speaking a form of trading,[1] is exempt from tax provided that both the following conditions are satisfied:

(1) the event is of a kind which falls within the exemption from VAT under Group 12 of Schedule 9 to VATA 1994; and

(2) the profits are given to charity or used for charitable purposes.

The rules relating to fundraising events and the various tax exemptions have been consolidated as a result of the 2000 Budget, so that an event which qualifies for exemption from VAT will also be exempt from income and corporation tax. This is to tidy up an anomaly that existed between the rules on one-off fundraising events in relation to the VAT exemption and the Inland Revenue's ESC C4.

Since 1 April 2000, if fundraising events, including participative events and events on the Internet, are run by a charity or by a voluntary organisation to raise funds for a charity, any profits from those events will be exempt from income and corporation tax provided the events qualify for exemption from VAT. The exemption applies not only to the actual profits of the event (obviously including any admission charges) but also to the proceeds from the sale of refreshments, advertising, programmes, raffle tickets, souvenirs, etc, provided they relate directly to the event and are sold at the event and not subsequently.

Any such fundraising event must not last for more than four days and the number of events allowed in any one year in any one location has been increased to 15 of each type or kind of event. However, for small-scale events the exemption will apply to any number of events, provided the gross weekly income from those events does not exceed £1,000. Charities and their advisers will no longer have to deal separately with the Inland Revenue and HM Customs and Excise to determine whether a fundraising event qualifies for exemption.[2]

The Finance Act 1995, s 138 amended ICTA 1988, s 505 specifically to remove the taxation of profits made from running a charity lottery. Effectively, the amendment exempts from tax under Schedule D profits accruing to a charity from a lottery, provided that the lottery, is promoted and conducted in accordance with the Lotteries and Amusements Act 1976, ss 3 or 5, or the Betting, Gaming, Lotteries and Amusements (Northern Ireland) Order 1985, arts 133 or 135. In addition, of course, the profits have to be applied solely for the charity's purposes.

---

1   ICTA 1988, s 832.

2   See further, Chapter 10.

4.3   SMALL-SCALE TRADING

Where a charity carries on a trade as part of its charitable purpose, the profits are normally exempt from tax. However, where the trade is purely for the purpose of raising funds, for example the sale of Christmas cards, then the profits generated will not usually be exempt from tax. With effect from 1 April 2000, a new tax exemption has been introduced[1] to cover the profits of certain small-scale trading activities carried on by charities that are not otherwise already exempt from tax. This may mean that many charities will no longer need to set up a trading company to carry on these activities.

This exemption will apply provided that the total turnover from all of the activities does not exceed the annual turnover limit or, if it does, that the charity had a *reasonable expectation* that it would not do so and all the profits are used solely for the purposes of the charity. The annual turnover limit is £5,000 or, if the turnover is greater than this, 25% of the charity's total gross incoming resources subject to a maximum limit of £50,000. Incoming resources are defined using the rules set out under charity accounting regulations and include the total receipts of the charity from all sources, eg grants, donations, legacies, investment income, income from trading activities, etc.

Example: The charity is selling Christmas cards as a fundraising trading activity and the total sales revenue is £4,500. If this is the only taxable fundraising trading activity, profits will be exempt from tax because the turnover does not

Trading Limits Flowchart

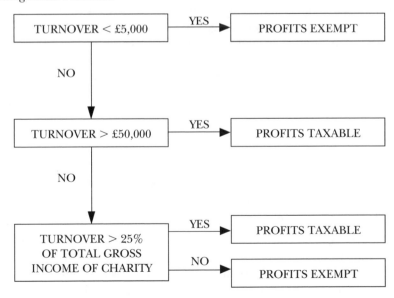

---

1   FA 2000, Pt III, ch II, s 46.

exceed £5,000. However, if the turnover from the sale of Christmas cards was £45,000 (which is less than the overall limit of £50,000) to qualify for the tax relief the total gross incoming resources of the charity would need to be greater than £180,000 (£180,000 at 25% = £45,000).

If the total turnover of the taxable fundraising trading activity for a tax year exceeds the annual turnover limit, the profits will still be exempt from tax, provided that the charity can show that, at the start of the tax year, it had a reasonable expectation that the turnover would not exceed the limit. The Inland Revenue Guidance Notes published with the Budget in March 2000 gave some examples of why this might be, eg the charity expected that turnover would be lower than it turned out to be, or the charity's incoming resources were lower than originally expected. Evidence might include minutes of meetings, copies of budgets, cashflow forecasts and prior year accounts.

4.4   MEANING OF 'TRADING'

In the last few years an increasing number of charities have set up trading activities in order to boost their income. Charity Christmas cards, mail-order catalogues, charity shops, sponsorship and affinity cards have now become very fashionable and are undoubtedly providing charities with considerable contributions towards fundraising. However, this is one area in which charities are most at risk in having to pay tax on the profits they make.

Before we look in detail at the exemptions offered by ICTA 1988, it is vital that we establish what is meant by trading. Tax under Schedule D Case I is charged in respect of any trade carried on in the UK or elsewhere. This seems simple enough. A trade can be quite easily identified, as for example, a corner shop, manufacturer of leather goods, electrician, etc, and obviously all these activities fall within Schedule D Case I. However, the Revenue's concept of trade is considerably widened by the definition of trade in ICTA 1988, s 832 as including: 'Every trade, manufacture, adventure or concern in the nature of trade'.

It is wise not to confuse 'trading' for income tax purposes with the VAT regulations on 'business'. The fact that a company or charity is not registered for VAT (because its activities are exempt) does not necessarily mean that those same activities will not be liable to income tax.

The question of what constitutes trading is one which has been the subject of examination by the courts and there are a large number of decided cases on the topic. Much guidance can be obtained from the decisions in these cases and this information may be important to charities in deciding whether or not some of their activities might constitute a trade. The three more important points, often described as the 'badges of trade', are summarised as follows:

- there must always be a profit motive in carrying out the activity, and the presence or absence of this particular factor would usually be extremely important. It will be unusual, if not difficult, for a charity undertaking business activity to argue that it was not intending to make a profit;
- any activity organised on a regular basis will be likely to be regarded as trade. However, there have been a number of important decisions, which covered differing situations, where the courts held that an isolated transaction of purchase and sale can be an adventure in the nature of trade. Factors such as the nature of the goods, what is done with those goods and the method of financing the transactions are particularly important;
- an adventure does not have to be an established trade provided that in its method of organisation and its activities it has the marks of a trading activity. So, on a very simple level, the village jumble sale could be regarded as being similar to a retail trading activity and therefore an adventure in the nature of trade. As such, its profit is taxable.

Occasionally, a single transaction of purchase and sale regarded by the charity as having the nature of a capital investment and yielding a capital gain, may nevertheless be considered by the Inland Revenue to be a trading profit. This is well illustrated by the case of the comedian Norman Wisdom[1] who having purchased a quantity of silver, as a hedge against inflation, made a profit on its disposal. He claimed the profit was capital, but the Inland Revenue was successful before the court in its contention that he had carried out an adventure in the nature of trade and should therefore be assessed to income tax.

Unfortunately, the definition in ICTA 1988, s 832 is not very helpful and it is worth noting that the words 'adventure or concern in the nature of trade' have been there for almost 200 years. One needs, therefore, to look elsewhere for help. The full facts and circumstances of the organisation of an activity must be taken into account before it can be said that a charity is trading. But many pitfalls can trap the unwary, and if matters have not been properly arranged, the profits from trading may not obtain the exemptions available.

Increasing use is being made by charities of the opportunity to sell donated goods through charity shops. Where exclusively donated goods are sold, the Inland Revenue will accept that this is not trading but purely the conversion of a donation into cash. However, once the charity begins to buy in goods for resale, that part of its activities would be regarded as trading and, where donated and purchased goods are sold side-by-side, it will certainly be necessary to apportion expenses.

Thus, where part of the charity's activities extend to the purchase of goods for resale, eg Christmas cards, which are then sold through the charity's shops, that part of the charity's activities would be regarded as trading and any profits

---

1   *Wisdom v Chamberlain* (1969) 45 TC 92.

generated would be subject to tax. It is therefore important to consider the nature of the goods being sold through the shops and identify an appropriate structure through which to operate.

4.5   TRADING EXEMPTIONS

The qualifications for exemption for trading are far tighter than those under other headings of the Taxes Acts, primarily ICTA 1988. The need to ensure that any profits are applied solely to the purposes of the charity remains uppermost, but at least one of two further conditions must also be fulfilled. They are that:

(1) the trade is exercised in the course of actually carrying out a primary purpose of the charity, for example where a medical relief charity runs a hospital; or

(2) the work in connection with the trade is mainly carried out by the beneficiaries of the charity, for example a workshop for the disabled run by a charity set up to provide work for disabled people.[1]

It would now be useful to look in detail at the exemption in s 505 of ICTA 1988, in particular s 505(1)(e). The exemption, where granted, applies to both corporation and income tax on trading income. The prime reason given for these restrictions, it is often alleged, has been to avoid unfair competition with non-charity traders. With the considerable growth in the charity world in recent years, could this view now be considered to be outdated?

4.5.1   'Primary purpose'

In considering whether the first of these conditions is being fulfilled, it is necessary to be quite clear about what are the main objects of the charity, as distinct from the purely peripheral ones. Sometimes, this will be obvious from the documents establishing the charity; and it would be advisable for anyone who is considering setting up a charity which will have a trading activity to ensure that the objects of the charity are clearly set out and that there can be no doubt that, in engaging in a trade, the charity is carrying out one of its main objects.

Compare the cases of two separate charities. The first, over 40 years ago in 1958 was *The Trustees of the Dean Leigh Temperance Canteen v CIR*,[2] which concerned the activities of a coffee shop set up to provide non-alcoholic and light refreshments at a time when there were 15 pubs around the market square. Despite the fact that the judge was highly critical of the founding document of the charity, the trading exemption was gained. The coffee shop was run by the trustees of the charity, which had been created to reduce the level of drunkenness in Hereford. The trust deed provided that any receipts of the business should

---

1   See ICTA 1988, s 505(1)(e).
2   (1958) 38 TC 315.

be applied to the running and maintenance of the coffee shop, to the provision of similar coffee shops elsewhere, or towards any other objects that tended to promote temperance. In actual fact, all the profits not required to run the coffee shops were either given to other temperance organisations or invested.

The decision in this case contrasts with that in 1903 of *Grove v YMCA*,[1] in which the profits of a restaurant opened to the public and run on commercial lines were held to be liable to tax. The objects of the YMCA included the spiritual, mental and social improvement of young men, and the association ran educational classes, a gymnasium and a publications department to those ends. The restaurant was opened to the public and the profits from the restaurant were used to subsidise the other activities. The court held that the restaurant was not carrying out a primary purpose of the charity and that therefore the profits were taxable.

Examples of primary purpose trading include:

- provision of educational services by a school;
- production of publications (relating to charitable objectives);
- regular conferences about the charity's objectives and how to achieve them;
- concerts held by a musical charity;
- educational courses;
- the provision of healthcare services by a hospital;
- the holding of an exhibition by an art gallery or museum;
- the provision of residential accommodation by a care charity;
- the sale of certain educational goods by an art gallery or museum; and
- the sale of tickets for a theatrical production staged by a theatre.

All the above examples are, of course, primary purpose trading. It is, however, clear that the exemption also extends to other trades which are not primary purpose activities but which are ancillary to the main objects of the charity. These are activities which are then deemed, in the view of the Inland Revenue, 'to be exercised in the course of the actual carrying out of a primary purpose'. Examples of these activities include:

- the sale of goods or services for the benefit of students by a school or college;
- the provision of a crèche for the children of students by a college or university;
- the sale of food and drink in a restaurant or bar to members of the audience by a theatre;
- the sale of confectionery, toiletries and flowers to patients and their visitors by a hospital or hospice; and
- the provision of accommodation to students by a school or college.

---

1   (1903) 4 TC 613.

Obviously, some trading may be a mix of primary purpose and non-primary purpose. As an example, the letting of accommodation for students during term time (primary purpose) and for tourists out of term (non-primary purpose) by a school or college; or the sale of food or drink in a theatre, restaurant or bar to both members of the audience (primary purpose trading) and the general public (non-primary purpose trading). Where this is the case, special care needs to be taken to ensure that the income and costs relating to the two types of trading are not mixed together.

It is likely that if the income and expenditure are mixed, the trade will not qualify as primary purpose *because* part of it is not related to a primary purpose. The activities cannot be extended, for example, where a museum sells a range of goods, some of which are not educational, a college rents accommodation for tourists during the holiday periods or a theatre restaurant or bar is open to members of the general public. Unless the amounts involved are small in themselves and the turnover of that part of the trade is less than 10% of the total turnover, the whole of the exemption for trading activity is lost. However, in practice, the Inland Revenue may include all the profits of the trade within the small scale trading exemption in the Finance Act 2000, provided it can be shown that the conditions have not been breached.

It is important therefore to distinguish between the sorts of activities, such as a charity shop or the sale of Christmas cards, which *enable* the charitable activities to be carried out on a wider basis, and activities, such as the production of publications and the organisation of conferences and cultural events, which fall *within the primary purposes*. There is often a very thin dividing line and each case needs close examination.

Unless extreme care is taken, the benefits to be gained from the trade may be lost and tax may become chargeable on *all* the trading profit. Additionally, in some cases the charitable status of the organisation may be put at risk. The 1980 report of the Charity Commissioners contained a lengthy section devoted to the trading activities of charities. In particular, paragraph 8 reads as follows:

> 'Drawing the line between the charity which is merely raising funds, and furthering its activities by trading and what is in substance a trading institution wearing a charitable mantle is not easy: each case must be considered on its own facts. There can be no objection to transitory and incidental trading by charities, for example, by jumble sales or by the running of shops to sell articles given by charitable minded people. But running a shop to make a profit from goods specifically bought for the purpose, or other trading on a permanent basis if permitted by the trust, might mean that the institution was not established for exclusively charitable purposes, and accordingly was not a charity within the meaning of sections 45 and 46 of the Charities Act 1960.'

One way of avoiding the problem is the setting up of a trading company (see **4.7**). An alternative way may have been to set up another charity whose main objective was to raise funds for the original charity that had set it up. The activities of such a charity (eg 'Friends of ...') had to be independent of the original charity and all the trading was tax-free as falling within the 'primary purpose' exemption. This was *not* really a serious option and is no longer recommended as the Charity Commission frowns upon it and the Inland Revenue also raised strong objections. It is mentioned for historic reasons only.

4.5.2 Work by beneficiaries

The second condition relevant to a trading exemption is that the work in connection with trade is mainly carried out by the beneficiaries of the charity. The sale of goods produced by handicapped people through a shop or mail-order catalogue would fall into this category. So, too, would the sale of goods produced by people in third-world countries supported by one of the overseas aid charities.

Problems can arise when this type of product forms only part of the throughput of a charity shop; it may then become a question of fact and degree to determine whether or not the exemption can be claimed. Other problems can also arise in determining whether the people doing the work are in fact beneficiaries of the charity and there may be dangers in drawing up the list of beneficiaries too narrowly. Care should be taken in drawing up the class of beneficiaries so that it is as wide as possible to take maximum advantage of exemption. Therefore, in the second example above, the list should include beneficiaries in all the third-world countries to ensure that all sources of goods are covered.

There have been a number of cases decided on this point and it is clear from the arrangement in the case of *The Convent of the Blessed Sacrament, Brighton v CIR*,[1] that one has to look at the substance of the case. In that case, the objects of the convent included the Christian education of young girls and the care of the sick. Convent members had taken vows of poverty and were entirely dependent upon the convent for their day-to-day requirements. In addition to their training in matters of religion, the nuns were also trained to teach in the convent school which was a fee-paying establishment.

The profits from this school were held to be exempt because the court refused to accept the Revenue's contention that the only beneficiaries of the charity were the pupils of the school. It held that the nuns were also beneficiaries of one of the purposes of the charity which was the sanctification of the Sisters by the worship of the Blessed Sacrament and by labour for the benefit of their fellow creatures. Thus, since they were involved in the running of the school, the profits were exempt.

This exemption is less used than that of primary purpose but some examples of trades commonly carried on by charities which will be exempt under the category of work by beneficiaries include:

—   a restaurant opened by students as part of a catering course;

---

1   (1933) 18 TC 76.

- a farm operated by students of an agricultural college;
- the sale of goods manufactured by the beneficiaries of a charity for people with disabilities.

4.6 PROFIT CALCULATION

Where a charity is carrying on a trade that is not exempt from tax (for whatever reason), the actual profit of the trade must be calculated in order to arrive at any tax liability. In calculating these profits, the charity will be able to deduct not only the direct expenditure of the trade but also a proportion of other indirect overheads which may be partly attributable, such as the running costs of the premises, salaries and administration costs.

It may also be possible to organise events amounting to trading activities so as to minimise the profit. This can be achieved by the charity setting a minimum charge and inviting voluntary donations, but it must be clearly stated that only the minimum charge need be paid, that further contributions are entirely discretionary and no additional benefit is secured by making the additional payment. In these circumstances, the income from which costs can be deducted in order to arrive at the taxable profits is only the minimum charge.

Where a charity makes a loss out of a trading activity it will be regarded as charitable expenditure if the activities are within the charity's objects. If they are not, the loss may be regarded as non-charitable expenditure, which can result in a general loss of the charity's exemption from tax. The Inland Revenue will normally only calculate the loss by reference to direct expenses in applying these provision.

4.7 TRADING COMPANY

The Charity Commissioners in their 1980 report positively favoured the idea of setting up a trading company:

> 'Where a charity wishes to benefit substantially from permanent trading for the purpose of fundraising, we advise that it does so through a separate non-charitable trading company, so that its charitable status is not endangered.'

However, the use of a trading company can be of assistance to any charity and not just to those which have problems in satisfying the conditions for exemption. It is necessary to ensure that arrangements are properly made so that none of the potential benefits are lost, therefore good legal and financial advice should always be sought. Four important steps to be considered in using a trading company are:

(1) setting up;

(2) funding;
(3) asset transfer;
(4) distribution of profits.

4.7.1 Setting up

The simplest type of company to set up is where the charity owns all the share capital, with the company carrying on the trade and agreeing to pay all the profits to the charity in some tax-efficient manner, details of which will be outlined at **4.7.4**. This means that the charity receives the profits as annual payments and, provided these payments are applicable and applied for charitable purposes, they will be exempt from income tax.

Before embarking upon this course, the charity must examine its trust deed to ensure that it is in fact able to use funds to invest in the company. The deed may have some specific prohibition or may have a requirement that the trustees should only put funds in sound investments which may not include a new trading venture. Long established trusts, in particular, may have this problem. New charities, which have a trading activity in mind, must ensure that they have specific provisions to allow investment accordingly. Obviously it is essential that the Memorandum and Articles of Association of the trading company allow it to covenant and make similar payments.

Taxation difficulties can arise under s 506 of ICTA 1988 which provides that charities will lose tax exemptions on a proportionate part of their income if they incur expenditure which is non-qualifying. Unfortunately, the list of qualifying investments contained in Pt I of Sch 20 to ICTA 1988 does not include unquoted shares. Therefore, approval for investment by a charity in a trading subsidiary will be required, not only from the Charity Commission but also from the Inland Revenue.

4.7.2 Funding

The funding of the company needs to be considered carefully and wherever possible the shares should be held wholly by the charity in order to avoid any problems which can be caused by close company legislation. The charity should avoid making loans to the company, since such a loan may not be for charitable purposes and could endanger its charitable status and tax exemptions. Any essential loan must be made on strictly commercial terms, most commonly by the debenture loan method. The Charity Commissioners (again, in their 1980 report) made it clear that the financial structures of the charity and the associated trading company should be kept distinct. Any attempt by a charity to prop up an unprofitable trading company would clearly not meet with the approval of the Charity Commissioners.

In fact, their 1988 report went further and said 'that normally funds needed to sustain or expand the activities of an associated trading company should be borne from commercial sources'.

This view created problems at the time for several charities and has never been satisfactorily resolved.

An investment is only a qualifying payment for tax purposes if it is made for charitable purposes only, for the benefit of the charity and not for the avoidance of tax. Unless it were in itself a commercially sound investment, ignoring the fact that the profits of the company were to be donated for charity, a loan or subscription for further shares by a charity would not fulfil these criteria. Therefore, charities should ensure that when a company is set up, it is provided with sufficient capital that it can donate all of its taxable profits each year and still stay in business. To resolve the problems, the charity should plan the setting up of a trading subsidiary carefully and prepare proper business plans, cashflow forecasts and profit projections.

Alternatively, the charity may decide that it would be better if the company did not donate all of its profits each year, so that sufficient funds will be retained by the company for working capital. This would leave part of the company's profits subject to corporation tax, but this may be preferable to the loss of future tax exemptions by the charity and the problems of an insolvent subsidiary.

Of course, the subsidiary can seek external financial assistance, but this could not take the form of equity investment as the company would then cease to be a wholly owned subsidiary of the charity. However, anyone providing an external loan to a company will look at the company's ability to make the necessary interest and loan repayments; therefore, they are unlikely to be willing to make a loan to a company which is unable to build up any reserves because it donates all of its taxable profits to its parent charity.

Any loan by the charity needs to be within Sch 20 to ICTA 1988 to be 'qualifying' expenditure; in particular, the Inland Revenue must be satisfied that the loan 'is made for the benefit of the charity and not for the avoidance of tax'. The Inland Revenue considers that a benefit to the charity will exist where:

(1)   the loan is adequately secured;
(2)   a commercial rate of interest is charged; and
(3)   there is a proper agreement showing terms of repayment.

In many cases (1) and (2) can present real difficulties. The company depends on the charity for its funding and it may therefore have no assets upon which the loan may be secured, nor might it have funds potentially available to meet a schedule of repayments.

The Charity Commissioners' Report in 1990 made reference to the case of *Minsham Properties v Price (Inspector of Taxes).*[1] This case concerned the administration of a loan account between a charitable company and one of its fully owned subsidiaries, engaged in trade. The charity had loaned the subsidiary £270,000 at interest. A loan account was opened in the books of the charity and its subsidiary; a charge for interest was periodically entered in the

---

1   [1990] STC 718.

account. The subsidiary claimed relief from corporation tax in respect of the interest charges under s 338 of ICTA 1988.

In order to qualify for relief, however, the interest should have been 'paid' out of the company's profits brought into charge to corporation tax. Both the Special Commissioners for income tax and the judge considered that the periodic journal entries, in which the interest was credited to the charity's account and debited to the subsidiary's account, did not amount to evidence that the interest had been paid. The entries were merely evidence that the interest had *not* been paid, and had, in consequence, been added to the debt. The relief from corporation tax was accordingly not available.

4.7.3 Asset transfer

Where the company's trade is carried on from owned/rented premises, these should be retained or put into the ownership/name of the charity, in order to maintain the statutory 80% business rate relief available to charities and to retain CGT exemptions which are not available to the trading company. However, the trading company must pay the parent charity for the use of such premises and for any other services provided to it by the parent charity.

4.7.4 Profit distribution

The company will be subject to corporation tax on its trading profit in the normal way (ICTA 1988, s 338). There used to be three ways in which a wholly owned trading subsidiary could pass both its profits to its parent charity and at the same time claim relief against its corporation tax liability. These were by covenant, dividend or Gift Aid. However, the 2000 Budget has changed that and now, provided all the profits are duly and correctly paid over to the charity as a qualifying donation within nine months of the end of the financial year of the trading subsidiary, no tax will become payable.

This is because the gross amount of the qualifying donation is allowed as a charge on income, as provided in ICTA 1988, s 338(1), which states that:

> 'in computing the corporation tax chargeable for any accounting period of a company any charges on income paid by the company in the accounting period, so far as paid out of the company's profits brought into charge to corporation tax, shall be allowed as deductions against the total profits for the period as reduced by any other relief from tax other than group relief.'

The Finance Act 2000 changed the previous regime where qualifying donations were paid net of tax, but retained the nine-month extension for payment set up in Finance Act 1997 (s 40(7)). However, it is not sufficient that the sum due should be legally payable. *It must actually be paid over within nine months of the end of the financial year to which it relates.* If a wholly owned subsidiary makes more than one separate payment of a qualifying donation to its parent charity, it does not matter if these are made after the subsidiary's year-end, provided they are made within the nine-month period allowed.

4.7.5   Profit retention

From 1 April 2000, the rate of corporation tax for companies with taxable profits of up to £10,000 is only 10%. Therefore, charities with trading subsidiaries are able to retain some of the profit without facing a significant tax bill in order to build up the working capital of the trading subsidiary. Funding the subsidiary with retained profits rather than borrowing from external sources, or indeed, in using the charity's own funds, may be the cheapest option.

In order to ease the climb from 10% corporation tax to the 20% rate for profit above £350,000, there is tapering relief at the rate of 2.5% applicable to profits between £10,001 and £50,000. Companies with profits between £50,001 and £300,000 will continue to pay tax at 20%. The full rate of corporation tax remains at 30%.

4.8   SPONSORSHIP

Sponsorship income may result from pure trading transactions, a genuine donation or a mixture of the two. Obviously, this has tax implications and trading transactions should be arranged through a subsidiary to avoid tax complications. Sponsorship is a thorny problem and liability will depend on the extent of the acknowledgement received by the sponsor.

Sponsorship can often take the form of a commercial organisation paying a substantial sum to enable the charity to mount an event. If the payment from the commercial organisation was made without expecting anything in return, the organisation itself may have difficulty in obtaining tax relief for the payment if it desires to do so. The usual arrangement, therefore, is that the company concerned will receive the benefit of advertising or something similar at the event. In these circumstances, it is likely that the charity will be considered to be providing a service for payment and that payment, as received by the charity, will be taxable.

When the acknowledgement to the sponsor is small and of a non-commercial nature, the charity may make it in the knowledge that it is unlikely that there would be any taxable benefit. However, if the acknowledgement is more substantial and of a commercial nature, eg advertising, it would become taxable.

Many sponsorship agreements fall between these two extremes. Often the value received by the sponsor is worth significantly less than the amount of sponsorship they give for the services they supply. If this is the case, it is often possible to split the sponsorship payment into two parts, though this must be done at the commencement of the agreement. The first part is regarded as the 'business' payment, with the expected value of the anticipated benefits, and the second is regarded as a voluntary donation that could be paid gross under Gift Aid.

When looking at a fundraising event of this sort, the Inland Revenue will examine the substance of the transaction and may conclude that the charity is selling advertising services. The taxation implications of sponsorship arrangements need to be considered carefully for both the charity and its sponsors.

Joint ventures can also lead to the taxation of intellectual property, in particular where a commercial organisation has the use of a charity's name and/or logo. This is often seen by the Inland Revenue as marketing by the charity of its name and logo to commercial organisations which then advertise their support for the charity. This could constitute a sale, leading to a taxable income.

It could also be interpreted as a supply of a trade mark or a sale of copyright. It is unlikely that provision of a name or logo for a single fundraising event would give rise to a tax liability. However, if there is a form of contract governing the use of the charity's name and its provision of promotional services to commercial organisations, the income would be assessable as trading income and would not be exempt.

The view of the Charity Commission is also relevant in this respect. In its 1991 report,[1] it made the point that 'the charity's name is a valuable asset' and went on to say in reference to the trustees that 'they must ensure that there is no misuse of the charity name nor any improper exploitation of its association with a commercial organisation and that arrangements made allow them to prevent any such misuse'.

Increasingly, sponsors are looking for some tangible reward for their sponsorship – a prominent display of the sponsor's name, the opportunity to advertise, complimentary tickets, etc. Sponsorship in these senses is very much a commercial activity. The sponsor would be seeking a deduction against its profits on the ground that the expenditure was incurred wholly and exclusively for the purposes of its trade. In such cases, the income in the hands of the recipient charity will be deemed to be a commercial transaction that could amount to a trade; after all, what the charity is doing is no different to, for instance, a motor-racing team which relies entirely on sponsorship to keep going. A charity cannot expect, and will not receive, special treatment. The tax and VAT[2] implications of this difficult concept require careful consideration.

---

1   Paragraph 107.
2   See further Chapter 10.

4.9 MISCELLANEOUS POINTS

4.9.1 Property transactions

The activity of buying and subsequently selling a piece of land or a building can give rise to serious tax problems for anyone who engages in it, including charities. The immediate reaction is to regard the profit made as being a capital gain liable to CGT or, in the case of a charity, exempt from tax. There will undoubtedly be many situations in which CGT is the proper basis of charge but two other possibilities may arise, both of which could cause real problems for a charity.

First, the Inland Revenue could argue that the activity of buying and selling property amounted either to the carrying on of a trade or to an adventure in the nature of trade, both of which are potentially assessable under Schedule D Case I. Typical factors which lend weight to such an argument are the length of time between purchase and sale, the method of financing the purchase, what was done to the property prior to sale and what motive was present in the original purchase. The charity held to be trading as a property dealer will probably have considerable difficulty in claiming exemption from income tax.

Secondly, the Inland Revenue has been using ICTA 1988, s 776 which is headed 'Transactions in Land: Taxation of Capital Gains'. This section is intended to tax profits on property transactions which have been arranged in order to give rise to a receipt of a capital nature. Usually there must be an intention by the taxpayer to acquire or develop a property with a view to making a profit on its disposal. An assessment under this section is in fact an assessment under Schedule D Case IV and would not be exempt under ICTA 1988, s 505.

Charities must therefore take great care before embarking on property transactions and, wherever possible, the use of a subsidiary trading company should be considered for any transactions which might have these sorts of implications.

Profits from a regular weekly dance held in the same free hall and donated to charity have been held by the courts to be taxable (*British Legion Peterhead Branch v CIR* (1953) 35 TC 509). However, the profit could be reduced by notional expenses which would have been incurred if the trade had been carried out on commercial lines (eg costs such as a hall rent, ticket printing, etc.). However, profits from ticket sales to regular concerts given by a charitable music festival which were used for the objects of a festival were held not to be taxable,[1] because they were deemed to be part of the charitable activity of carrying out a primary purpose under what is now s 505 of ICTA 1988.

---

1   *CIR v Glasgow Music Festival Association* (1926) 11 TC 154.

4.9.2   Affinity cards

Profits from affinity card schemes have also come under close scrutiny. Although negotiations with the Inland Revenue and Customs and Excise diminished the liability to both corporation tax and VAT, there still remains a charge. It is therefore advisable to put these transactions through a subsidiary company, provided that this can be done legitimately. Obviously, all agreements with the third party (eg bank/building society) must be entered into by the trading subsidiary, *not* the charity.

4.9.3   Licensing a charity's name

A charity may licence its name in exchange for a royalty. However, activities of this nature can be charged to income tax under Case VII of Schedule D, from which no exemption is given under s 505 of ICTA 1988. Therefore, income tax will be payable in respect of such receipts by a charity. However, in some cases, the royalty will be treated as an annual payment, being Schedule D Case III income, which is exempt. This will apply where the charity has done nothing to earn the royalty and it is pure profit in its hands.

4.10   CONCLUSION

Finally, a few cautionary words of warning, as Shakespeare said in 'As You Like It': 'You'll be whipped for taxation one of these days'.

Or as Prince Philip said slightly more recently, in the days of Chancellor Lawson: 'All money nowadays seems to be produced with a natural homing instinct for the Treasury'.

Chapter 5

CAPITAL TAXES AND STAMP DUTY

'He that defers his charity until he is dead is, if a man weighs it
rightly, rather liberal of another man's than his own.'

Francis Bacon, Collection of sentences no 55

5.1 CAPITAL TAXES

5.1.1 Historical background

The two UK taxes which aim specifically at taxing capital are capital gains tax (CGT) and inheritance tax (IHT). Capital is a word with a multiplicity of meanings, but in this context we will adopt the sense with which the Finance Act 1975 defined a person's estate:

> 'a person's estate is the aggregate of all the property to which he is beneficially entitled.'[1]

The holders of such stores of wealth have long been seen by money-hungry governments as fit targets for taxation. The traditional manner in which they relieved the holder of some of his assets was to charge a proportion of their value. One example was the Land Tax, by which the government took 4 shillings in the pound (20%) of the value of a person's total assets. The problem with such methods was the valuation of the assets: how regular was it to be and on what basis?

An alternative method of releasing some of the assets into the hands of the government was to tax transfers of assets. In an age when the bureaucracy of tax collection was scanty and primitive it would have been difficult to tax all transfers, but there was one compulsory transfer which it was impossible to hide: death. Taxes on the value of assets transferred at death were introduced in England in 1694, and not surprisingly became known as death duties. By 1894, when it was decided to reform them, there were five different types: probate duty, legacy duty, succession duty, account duty, and temporary estate duty. The Finance Act 1894 introduced estate duty as the key tax on death transfers. It began as just that but, by the end of its life, its tax base had been extended to include gifts made in the seven years before death also. If a person wished to give assets to a charity, or indeed anyone else, an *inter vivos* gift, made at least seven years before death meant that the assets would leave the estate and would not be included on death. However, if the transfer was made on death (as

---

1   FA 1975, s 23.

a result of a will), or within seven years of death, the assets would be deemed still part of the estate on death and thus, taxable.

It was only late in the life of estate duty that any concessions were made towards the encouragement of charitable giving. The Finance Act 1969 excluded gifts for charitable purposes from the estate if they were made more than one year before the donor's death.[1] The Finance Act 1972 extended donor relief by removing gifts and settlements of up to £50,000 from the charge, thus for the first time allowing relief for charitable transfers on death.[2]

The successor to estate duty, capital transfer tax (CTT), took over these concessions and extended them. In Sch 6, para 10 to the Finance Act 1975 transfers of value were exempt:

> 'to the extent that the values transferred by them –
>   (a)   are attributable to property which is given to charities; and
>   (b)   so far as made on or within one year of the death of the transferor, do not exceed £100,000.'

Paragraph 10(b) continued the penalisation of gifts to charities made on or within one year of death if over a certain amount, now twice as much as the concession in Finance Act 1972. CTT differed from estate duty in one major way: it was a tax on all gifts, not just those within the last seven years of life. The essence of the tax is well described by McCutcheon and Whitehouse:[3]

> 'CTT was in many ways a brilliantly simple tax in conception since it was based upon the fundamental premise that all gifts of property, whether made inter vivos or on death, should be cumulated together and progressive rates of tax applied to the ever-increasing cumulative total. In every sense, therefore, it was a cradle to grave tax, with the passing of a taxpayer's property on death being the final gift.'

5.1.2   Inheritance tax

From its beginning, gifts to charity were protected: the fall in value of an individual's estate as a result of a gift to charity was not taxable, whereas most other gifts were. The subsequent reforms of CTT by Chancellors Howe and Lawson, finally resulting in the renaming of CTT as inheritance tax, improved the full vigour of the original conception by making most gifts potentially exempt transfers (PETs) if made more than seven years before death, thereby restoring that key feature of the old estate duty, the lottery of longevity. PETs and another planning mechanism, the deed of variation, have considerably

---

1   FA 1969, Sch 17, para 9.
2   FA 1972, s 121 and Sch 26.
3   BD McCutcheon and C Whitehouse, *McCutcheon on Inheritance Tax* 3rd edn (Sweet & Maxwell, 1988).

reduced the yield of IHT. Deeds of variation effectively permit a will to be re-written in tax-favourable terms, thanks to s 142 of IHTA 1984.[1]

The key section for donors to charities, IHTA 1984, s 23(1), provides:

'Transfers of value are exempt to the extent that the values transferred by them are *attributable to* property which is given to *charities.*'

The words in italics may need a little clarification. '*Attributable to*' means that the exemption extends to the whole value of the property transferred, not just to its value in the hands of the charity when the values differ, as they might do where a person reduces a majority holding of shares to a minority holding by giving some shares to a charity. The value of the shares in the charity's hands will be considerably less than their value as part of a majority holding. In this case the value as part of the majority holding will be exempt from IHT. '*Charities*' is defined as it is in ICTA 1988. The definition is found in s 506:

'*charity* means any body of persons or trust established for charitable purposes only.'

The rest of s 23 is taken up with four subsections providing anti-avoidance measures, expressed in the customary language of such measures. There is also one definition subsection. Each aims to remove the exemption granted in subs (1) if the transfer is of a certain type. If this removal occurs then the transfer in most cases would revert to being a PET, thus softening the blow. All the subsections were present, in a slightly different form, in the original legislation, the Finance Act 1975 (FA 1975),[2] except for subs (4) which was introduced by the Finance Act 1976 (FA 1976).[3] Each subsection will be discussed as they occur in the legislation, which proceeds as follows:

'(2) Subsection (1) shall not apply in relation to property if the testamentary or other disposition by which it is given –
  (a)   takes effect on the termination after the transfer of value of any interest or period, or
  (b)   depends on a condition which is not satisfied within twelve months after the transfer, or
  (c)   is defeasible;
and for this purpose any disposition which has not been defeated at a time twelve months after the transfer of value shall be treated as not being defeasible (whether or not it was capable of being defeated before that time).'

The purpose of subs (2) is to remove exemption from a gift to charity which does not take place immediately but has some kind of long-term condition attached, or where the asset goes to someone else first, or where it is not a bona fide gift; for example, where a house is gifted to a person on condition that the house passes to a registered charity on his death.

---

1   For details of the various planning possibilities available with these see P Laidlow, *Tax Planning for Post-Death Variations* (Tolleys, 1993).
2   FA 1975, Sch 6, Pt II, para 15.
3   FA 1976, s 95(2)(bb)(cc).

The definition of 'defeasible' according to Jowitt[1] is:

> 'capable of being annulled or abrogated. An estate or interest in property is said to be defeasible when it is subject to be defeated by the operation of a condition subsequent or conditional limitation.'

The next subsection traverses similar ground:

> '(3) Subsection (1) shall not apply in relation to property which is an interest in other property if –
>> (a) that interest is less than the donor's, or
>> (b) the property is given for a limited period;
>
> and for this purpose any question whether an interest is less than the donor's shall be decided at a time twelve months after the transfer of value.'

This refers to the situation where the asset gifted is only a part of, or an interest in the full asset owned by the donor; for example, where a donor grants to charity, *gratis*, a 90-year lease on a freehold property which he owns. The property will eventually revert to the donor: he is not giving up his full rights in the property and thus falls foul of subsection (3). If a donor assigns a leasehold to a charity, *gratis*, but does not own the freehold, this should not fall foul of subsection (3).

The next, rather bulky, subsection aims at preventing reservation of benefits in favour of the donor, and was introduced by FA 1976:

> '(4) Subsection (1) above shall not apply in relation to any property if –
>> (a) the property is land or a building and is given subject to an interest reserved or created by the donor which entitles him, his spouse or a person connected with him to possession of, or to occupy, the whole or part of the land or building rent-free or at a rent less than might be expected to be obtained in a transaction at arm's length between persons not connected with each other, or
>> (b) the property is not land or a building and is given subject to an interest reserved or created by the donor other than –
>>> (i)   an interest created by him for full consideration in money or money's worth, or
>>> (ii) an interest which does not substantially affect the enjoyment of the property by the person or body to whom it is given;
>
> and for this purpose any question whether property is given subject to an interest shall be decided as at a time twelve months after the transfer of value.'

The main reservation of benefit provisions as they now stand were introduced by FA 1986 (s 102 and Sch 20) but the legislation in relation to charitable donations antedates them by 10 years. McCutcheon describes the rules behind the prevention of a reservation of benefit as follows:

> 'Their effect is to make it difficult in many cases for a taxpayer to make a tax-efficient gift if the circumstances and/or terms are such that he may still derive some benefit from the subject matter of the gift.'

---

1   *Jowitt's Dictionary of English Law* 2nd edn, J Burke (ed) (1977).

Section 23(4)(a) is reasonably self-evident; s 23(4)(b) less so. In the latter case, an asset can be given subject to an interest so long as it does not substantially affect the charity's enjoyment, or its beneficiaries' enjoyment, of the asset. Thus, where a painting is donated to an art education charity, but it is stipulated that it remains over the donor's fireplace, this is likely to substantially affect the beneficiaries' enjoyment of the painting, and thus falls outside the exemption in s 23(1).

The last substantive subsection (s 23(5)) reiterates the condition, expressed in the income tax exemptions, that donations should be applied for charitable purposes only:

'(5) Subsection (1) above shall not apply in relation to property if it or any part of it may become applicable for purposes other than charitable purposes ...'

Care might need to be taken where an asset is donated to the trading company of a charity and is used there. The asset is being used, not for charitable purposes but to generate cash.

The above paragraphs comprise the legislative background. How can the relief from IHT be used most effectively? One's estate must be worth more than £234,000 (2000/2001) for IHT to be payable, the death rate being 40%. Only the excess above £234,000 is charged. Legacies and bequests to charities on death out of the chargeable estate will therefore be exempt from 40% tax.

It has been suggested that the most effective way to use the IHT reliefs is in combination with income tax reliefs. One such scheme proceeds as follows. The testator makes a pecuniary legacy to an individual and expresses a wish that this legacy should be given to charity, making it a so-called precatory legacy. If that individual makes the gift to charity within two years of the death then s 143 of IHTA 1984 gives it relief from IHT. To encourage the individual to make the gift, he will be eligible for higher-rate relief because the gift can be treated as a Gift Aid payment. The recipient charity will be happy because it will be able to reclaim basic-rate tax on the receipt; so everyone will be happy except the Revenue.

A possible objection to such a scheme is that a precatory gift is not really a gift at all because its destination is stipulated. To be valid for Gift Aid purposes the gift must be gratuitous. Another possible objection is that the scheme constitutes a preplanned arrangement to avoid tax and as such open to attack under the *Furniss v Dawson*[1] doctrine, ie that the substance of a series of transactions can be distinguished from the legal form in which they are expressed, and if their purpose is tax avoidance, the legal form should be ignored. However, Kessler is confident this would not succeed.[2] The Revenue's view, apparently, is that the IHT saving is a benefit to the donor, which then prevents the use of Gift Aid. As yet, no test cases have arisen to the authors' knowledge.

---

1   *Furniss v Dawson* [1982] STC 267 at 73, 87.
2   This scheme was suggested by James Kessler in the *New Law Journal*, 5 October 1990, pp 1391–1392.

The discussion above has concentrated on donor reliefs. What is the IHT situation in relation to a charitable trust itself? IHT is not chargeable on companies but is chargeable on certain types of trust. A charitable trust is a special form of discretionary trust, ie a trust where the trustees have absolute discretion as to the application of funds, so long as it is within the terms of the charitable objects. The relevant legislation is contained in s 58, s 70 and s 76 of IHTA 1984. Section 76 states that IHT shall not be charged on property which becomes:

> 'property held for charitable purposes only without limit of time (defined by a date or otherwise).'

Section 58 excludes property held for charitable purposes only from the rules taxing settlements without interests in possession. In the rather special circumstances where property is held on charitable trusts for a limited period, s 70 is relevant. There will be a charge to IHT when the property ceases to be so held 'otherwise than by virtue of an application for charitable purposes'. Thus, the trust can divest itself of its property by applying it for a charitable purpose and avoid IHT, but not if the property passes to non-charitable ownership. The tax charge is calculated on the fall in value of the settlement before and after the transfer of the property. The calculation of the actual tax rate used is complex and is contained in s 70(6)–(10).

5.1.3 Capital gains tax

We will consider next, the reliefs available to charities themselves against their capital gains. CGT is charged on individuals and trusts; the chargeable gains of companies are charged to tax via corporation tax, not through CGT. However, the reliefs contained in the CGT legislation are available to charities which are incorporated.

Charities were favourably treated from the introduction of CGT: s 35 of the Finance Act 1965 (FA 1965) introduced the provision (which is now s 256(1) of the Taxation of Chargeable Gains Act 1992) relieving charities themselves from CGT on their gains:

> 'a gain shall not be a chargeable gain *if it accrues to a charity* and is applicable and applied for charitable purposes.'

This relief was introduced before the addition of indexation allowances; therefore 'the gain' to be applied and applicable for charitable purposes is the unindexed gain. This will clearly be higher than the chargeable gain, so care is required if full relief is to be enjoyed. If only the chargeable gain is applied for charitable purposes, there would, in theory, be a chargeable gain on an amount equal to the indexation allowance. This amount would then be eligible for its own indexation allowance. In practice, it should not be too difficult to ensure that the whole gain is applicable and applied for charitable purposes.

A gain will 'accrue to' a charity if it occurs as a result of the disposal of an asset beneficially owned by the charity, or held on charitable trusts.

The gains would not have to be spent on specific charitable projects: expenditure of gains on the regular administrative expenses of the charity will be a valid application. Clearly, these are likely to accrue only gradually, so an intention to use the gain for these purposes should be made explicit. Earmarking of gains for future identifiable projects should also be valid as applicable and to be applied in the future. Simply leaving the gain in qualifying investments as defined by Sch 20 to ICTA 1988, such as a normal bank deposit account, would not be sufficient to qualify for relief.

It is important to remember that the restrictive provisions of ICTA 1988, ss 505(3)–(8) and s 506 apply equally to gains as to income. It is necessary to consider the purposes for which income and gains together have been applied when answering the series of questions on qualifying expenditure set out in Chapter 2 at **2.3.2**. Care needs to be taken because gains tend to be large and irregular, disturbing the normal pattern of expenditure, but they can be planned.

Where a charity is a trust, specific problems will arise in relation to capital gains if the trust loses its charitable status, or if assets which were held on charitable trusts cease to be so held. In the normal course of events, charitable trusts enjoy perpetuity and it is very unusual for such a trust to lose its charitable status, except when it is voluntarily wound-up. A more likely situation might be where someone is tempted to place assets temporarily on charitable trusts in connection with a tax avoidance scheme. Specific anti-avoidance legislation, dating from the Finance Act 1965, is aimed at discouraging this and is found in s 256(2) of TCGA 1992:

> 'If property held on charitable trusts ceases to be held on charitable trusts –
> (a)   the trustees shall be treated as if they had disposed of, and immediately reacquired, the property for a consideration equal to its market value, any gain on the disposal treated as not accruing to the charity, and
> (b)   if and so far as any of that property represents, directly or indirectly, the consideration for the disposal of assets by the trustees, any gain accruing on that disposal shall be treated as not having accrued to a charity,
> and an assessment to capital gains tax chargeable by virtue of paragraph (b) above may be made at any time not more than 3 years after the end of the year of assessment in which the property ceases to be subject to charitable trusts.'

This subsection deems the trustees to have made a disposal when none has actually taken place. The market value of the assets concerned will be compared with their original cost, plus indexation allowance when transferred to the charity. The deemed gain, which is not eligible for indexation allowance because it is a deemed and not an actual disposal, is assessable on the trustees, and becomes an actual tax bill.

The purpose of s 256(2)(b), which not be immediately apparent, is as follows. If an asset held in the charity at winding up is itself the final result of an accumulation of exempt capital gains, then s 256(2)(b) allows the Revenue to tax all these gains retrospectively. For example, if an asset is gifted to a charity, then sold, and the gain is reinvested in another asset; where the second asset remains in the trust on winding up, the gain, measured as the difference between final market value and original cost, plus indexation when gifted to the charity, will all be taxable. It does not matter what form the asset takes: it could even be in the form of cash. To avoid such a retrospective charge it is advisable to ensure there are no assets remaining in the trust on winding up.

The original CGT legislation introduced by the Finance Act 1965 did not contain any relief for donors to charities. This relief was introduced in 1972 by the then Chancellor of the Exchequer, Anthony Barber, and the provision has not changed materially since.[1] The relief is given where a disposal to a charity is made 'otherwise than under a bargain at arm's length', ie a gift, or transfer for lower than market value.

In this context, there are two situations to consider. First, where the asset is either given *gratis* to the charity or is sold to it at less than cost; and secondly, where the asset is sold to the charity at an amount higher than cost but lower than market value.

In the first situation, the deemed value of the proceeds will produce neither gain nor loss for the donor. In other words, the deemed proceeds will be equal to the allowable deductions plus indexation allowance, thus no charge accrues to the donor, nor does an allowable loss occur. In the second situation, there will be a chargeable gain for the donor to the extent that actual proceeds exceed allowable deductions, with indexation allowance taken into account.

At what value is the charity deemed to have acquired the asset? In the first situation, the amount will be the original allowable deduction of the person who gave the asset, that is, the cost of the asset to the donor, plus the indexation allowance on disposal to the charity: that is, the deemed proceeds. In the second situation, it will be the amount the charity paid for the asset, ie the actual proceeds.

CGT reliefs

When settlements terminate in favour of a charity there are reliefs available. When a life tenant dies and the residue passes to a charity, the charity is deemed to acquire the assets at their market value on termination. If the termination is not due to the death of a life tenant the disposal to the charity is treated as having been made at no gain and no loss, as in the first situation above.

How useful are these CGT reliefs? If we consider a situation where there is a choice of reliefs open to a donor, we will see that income tax reliefs tend to be more attractive. The first example concerns an asset that is neither shares nor securities.

Croesus wishes to benefit his favourite charity and has earmarked an unpleasant but very valuable antique for this purpose. The market value of the

---

1   Originally FA 1972, s 119 and now TCGA 1992, s 257.

antique is £30,000; it cost Croesus £5,000. Croesus is unsure of the most tax-efficient way of transferring the benefit of the antique to the charity. He has made no chargeable gains and is a higher rate income tax payer.

If Croesus were simply to give the antique to the charity he would not have to pay CGT on it. He would still have his annual CGT exemption of £7,200 (2000/2001) to use against other chargeable gains. The gift is a potentially exempt transfer for IHT purposes and no IHT will be payable if he survives seven years. There would be no effect on his income tax position. The charity would dispose of the antique and gain £30,000 in cash.

If Croesus were to dispose of the antique himself and then give the cash to the charity, the following tax effects occur. First, he will have made a chargeable gain, thus:

	£
Proceeds	30,000
Cost	(5,000)
Unindexed gain	25,000
Indexation (say 77.5%)	(3,875)
Chargeable gain	21,125
Annual exemption	(7,200)
	13,925
CGT at 40%	5,570

If Croesus gifts the cash, he received from the sale via Gift Aid to the charity, the amount he gives will be deemed to be the net amount. The charity will be able to reclaim the tax deducted on this amount, thus:

	£
Net amount received from Croesus	30,000
Tax reclaimed from Revenue (22/78)	8,461
Total benefit to charity	38,461

Because Gift Aid charges are allowable against higher rate tax, Croesus will be able to reduce the amount of higher rate tax he would otherwise have to pay, thus:

Reduction of higher rate tax = 18% × £38,461 = £6,923

A cost benefit analysis of the two strategies looks like this:

(a) **Straight gift to charity**

	£
Benefit to charity	30,000

Cost to Croesus	nil
Total benefit	30,000

(b) **Disposal by Croesus**

Benefit to charity	38,461
Cost to Croesus (CGT)	(5,570)
Use of annual exemption	
(40% × £7,200)	(2,880)
Benefit to Croesus (HRIT)	6,923
Total benefit	36,934
In favour of strategy (b)	£6,934

The important point regarding charity tax reliefs is that they should be considered together, as exemplified by the IHT example above.

As we have seen in Chapter 3, the Finance Act 2000 introduced a new relief for gifts of quoted shares to a charity. This is known as Share Gift Relief.

The benefit of the relief is applicable wholly to the donor in that the market value of the shares will be fully deductible from total income. Relief is therefore given at the donor's marginal rate of income tax. The deduction includes any incidental costs of disposal. In technical terms the deduction is treated as a charge on income. The donor will still be eligible for CGT relief under s 257 of TCGA 1972.

This new relief is more beneficial than the use of Gift Aid described above for Croesus. The difference is that the relief is not shared between the donor and the charity but goes wholly to the donor. This relief marks a new departure for UK charity tax reliefs and it will be interesting to see whether the range of eligible assets is extended. There have already been demands that unquoted shares in general should be included.

5.2   STAMP DUTY

Stamp duty in its present slender form does not justify a chapter to itself and there is a certain logic in placing it with the capital taxes. Stamp duty is a tax on instruments transferring title to assets. The early forms of death duties were a variation on stamp duty, whereby duty was charged on the probate documents transferring title after death.

Stamp duty was introduced into the UK in 1694 in the reign of William III to pay for his wars and is the second oldest of the taxes under consideration; the oldest tax is rates on property (see Chapter 7). It is a curious and now rather obscure tax, being in essence a tax on values transferred by certain documents, known as 'instruments'. It is the documents of transfer that are taxable, not persons. It owes its longevity possibly to the fact that it is not easy to avoid as long as certain documents are essential in the legal transfer of property. Despite its obscurity, it brings in more money than either CGT or IHT. In terms of statute law, there have been Consolidation Acts since 1694, the last ones being the Stamp Act 1891 and the Stamp Duties Management Act 1891. These two statutes remain the principal Acts, as amended by 112 years of Finance Acts.

Let us consider how stamp duty works before we consider charitable exemptions. Stamp duty is charged on the value transferred by certain types of instruments, ie documents transferring title in property. The value taxed is the gross amount including VAT. The number of taxable instruments has declined over the years, and these days the most important are transfers of shares (whose days are apparently numbered), land transactions and sales of businesses. Until 1970, cheques were taxable instruments and stamp duty was charged on the value of the cheque.

The rate of the tax depends on the type of instrument being charged. Certain instruments are subject to a fixed charge, such as 50p per document; others to an '*ad valorem*' amount, calculated by reference to the value of the consideration recorded on the instrument. Current stamp duty rates are 50p fixed; 0.5% *ad valorem* rate on sale of shares; and 1–4% *ad valorem* on transfers of other property. Stamp duty is chargeable in the case of land and property only if the transfer value is over £60,000. The rate is 1% up to a value of £250,000; 3% from £250,001 to £500,000; and 4% from £500,001 (FA 2000).

Payment of the duty is generally made before or shortly after execution of the instrument, ie the time when the instrument takes legal effect. There is no general rule as to who should pay the tax, though in reality the purchaser is usually the person who pays it because the purchaser is generally liable for penalties for late stamping. These penalties for late stamping, are civil, non-stamping is never a criminal offence, unlike serious transgressions against almost all other taxes. The main sanction for non-payment of stamp duty is that an instrument will not be admissible in any civil action unless properly stamped, that means the civil law will not recognise it as a valid transfer.

5.2.1 Exemptions from stamp duty

For most of the life of stamp duty, charities did not enjoy any particular special status, though transfers for the building of churches were exempted in 1822, and transfers for the consecration of graveyards were exempted in 1867. Charities in general had to wait until the Finance Act 1982 (FA 1982), which states that stamp duty is not charged on 'any conveyance, transfer or lease made or agreed to be made to a charity'.[1]

---

1   FA 1982, s 129.

This exemption covers transfers of property to charities, but not transfers by charities to non-charities. Such transfers are not exempt, but the purchaser will usually pay the tax. The 1982 exemption covers the payment of stamp duty on such transfers to charity, but for this exemption to apply, the instrument concerned has to be 'adjudicated'. This means that the Revenue has to formally assess that the exemption applies. Thus, a stamp certifying the exemption will need to be applied to the instrument. To obtain this, the instrument should be sent to the Office of the Controller of Stamps in Worthing.

5.2.2   Stamp duty reserve tax

Stamp duty reserve tax (SDRT) is a separate tax from stamp duty and was introduced by FA 1986. Its aim is to tax certain transfers of securities which fall outside the scope of stamp duty, in particular, transactions which do not involve the use of transfer documents, or where there is no change in the registered ownership of the shares. Charities are exempted from SDRT by FA 1987, Sch 7, para 6(1), which states that agreements to transfer securities to charities are exempt.

Chapter 6

EMPLOYMENT TAX RESPONSIBILITIES FOR CHARITIES

'What profit hath he that worketh in that wherein he laboureth?'

Ecclesiastes 3.9

6.1   INTRODUCTION

The responsibilities of a charity in relation to its own employees are in the main no different from those of any other organisation which employs workers. However, a charity bears additional responsibilities as a trust and can less afford to ignore them because payment of any penalties and interest to the Inland Revenue might lead to complaints of breach of trust. At the very least, such payments will deplete hard-won charity resources. It is worth considering these responsibilities because of the extra dangers they may pose to charities without strong administrative experience.

6.2   PAYE AND NICs

The employer's responsibilities lie primarily in relation to the Pay As You Earn (PAYE) scheme, by which income tax and national insurance contributions (NICs) are collected by the employer on behalf of the employee and paid over to the Revenue. Both the Employer Compliance and National Insurance sections of the Revenue have in recent years devoted more resources to the policing of the PAYE/NIC scheme, in particular through the use of teams who may descend on organisations with little warning. Charities are as likely to be visited by such teams as any other organisation, so it is important to ensure that the scheme is being operated correctly at all times. Indeed there is clear evidence that charities have recently become the particular target for visits.

The statutory authority for the PAYE scheme lies in ss 203– 203L of ICTA 1988, the core of which is as follows:

'(1)   On the making of any payment of, or on account of, any income assessable to income tax under Schedule E, income tax shall, subject to and in accordance with regulations made by the Board under this section, be deducted or repaid by the person making the payment, notwithstanding that when the payment is made no assessment has been made in respect of the income and notwith-standing that the income is in whole or in part income for some year of assessment other than the year during which the payment is made.

(2)   The Board shall make regulations with respect to the assessment, charge, collection and recovery of income tax ...'

The regulations referred to[1] establish the detailed operation of the scheme. The statutory authority for the collection of NICs in a similar way is the Social Security Contributions and Benefits Act 1992, Sch 1 para 6, with the detailed administrative procedures being regulated by SI 1979/591. It is not the intention here to cover all the detailed requirements of the scheme. These can be found in the literature produced by the Revenue.[2] We propose to concentrate on the key danger areas where a charity can be exposed to penalties, and we shall do this by exploring some of the concepts of Schedule E.

Income tax is charged under Schedule E on the emoluments of an office or employment. An 'office' is a position existing independently of the person currently occupying it, eg Richard Harries holds the office of Bishop of Oxford, and so is an office-holder rather than an employee of the Church of England. The difference between an office and an employment now has little significance. The basis of assessment of Schedule E is amounts received in the tax year, not amounts earned, so a bonus for the two years to 31 March 2001 but received on 8 April 2001 will be taxed in 2001/2002, not 2000/2001. The tax will be collected under the PAYE scheme at the end of April 2001. The tax office dealing with the employer's responsibilities for employees' tax will not be FICO (which deals only with the charity's own tax affairs), but a PAYE tax office depending on where the charity is situated.

If a person receives income which is determined to be Schedule E income, the payer is responsible for deducting the tax and paying it to the Revenue. If a person is in receipt of income under any other Schedule, the employer is under no obligation to account for the tax: this is a matter between the individual and the Revenue.[3] Employees' earnings are subject to national insurance. This is also collectable by the employer, and is paid to the Revenue at the same time as income tax. National insurance contributions are discussed in more detail at **6.2.3**.

The key terms that require definition are:

(1) employment – when is a person an employee? (this relevant for both Schedule E and NICs);
(2) emoluments – what is taxable under Schedule E?
(3) earnings – what is subject to National Insurance?

---

1   SI 1993/744.
2   See, in particular, Employer's Quick Guide to PAYE & NICs (IR Leaflet CWG1); Employer's Further Guide to PAYE & NICs (IR Leaflet CWG2); Expenses and Benefits: A Tax Guide (IR Booklet 480); Employee Travel: A Tax NICs Guide for Employers (IR Booklet 490).
3   A case which discussed this area is *IRC v Herd* (1993) STC 436.

6.2.1 Employment

The Revenue look very critically at people claiming to be self-employed because the self-employed tax regime is less favourable for the tax authorities, most obviously so in terms of cashflow and employers' National Insurance.

From the charity's point of view, if a person is categorised as an employee, the charity as employer will be responsible for tax on the employee's emoluments paid by the charity. If the charity treats someone wrongly as self-employed and does not deduct tax and NIC under the PAYE scheme, the consequences can be serious. The charity could find itself having to pay tax interest and penalties which it may not be able to recover from the employee. The charity should not therefore simply accept someone's word that they are self-employed. Whether they are or not is a question to be determined by looking at the nature of their work relationships. Furthermore, the worker's relationship with the Revenue (has he paid his tax?) could be relevant in determining the final bill.

In the case of charities, it may be that problems of determining whether a person is employed or self-employed are more likely to arise than in normal business, because charities are often less cohesive organisations – they have a more fluid nature, and they come and go in response to needs. The relationship of master and servant may be more difficult to distinguish in an organisation that does not have strict management structures.

Whether a person is employed or self-employed has significant consequences for the income tax and National Insurance liability of the employee and employer, in particular:

(a) Tax is payable under the PAYE system much earlier than Schedule D Case I or II tax on self-employed earnings. Under PAYE, tax is payable at the end of the earnings period, weekly or monthly as the case may be. This cash flow advantage of PAYE from the government's point of view is of course one reason why it was introduced.
(b) The expenses of a self-employed person are generally more easily deductible than the expenses incurred by an employee.
(c) An employee will be subject to the more expensive Class 1 NICs. Self-employed people pay the lower Class 2 and 4 NICs.
(d) The employer must pay secondary Class 1 contributions on cash earnings and Class 1A contributions on most benefits for employees but not for the self-employed.

Who is an employee?
Employment exists in general terms when there is a legal relationship of master and servant. Whether this relationship exists may be evidenced by a contract of employment or implied by conduct. It is, however, important to note that a written statement declaring that a person is self-employed, and responsible for their own tax, has no weight if the true nature of the working relationship indicates employment. Each case should be decided on the facts but the following indicate the sort of tests that could be applied in a charity context:

– Where the written terms of the agreement between the charity and the person indicate that it is a contract of service, this will indicate employment; whereas a contract for services indicates self-employment. This test may not be conclusive.

– Can the person decide on where, when and how the work is performed? For instance, are working hours and location of work contractually laid down?

– Is there a 'master/servant' relationship in that there are disciplinary procedures etc which indicate employment?

– Is the individual part of the charity's organisation, eg part of the management reporting structure?

– Does the individual provide his own equipment – eg computer? (Own car is not particularly relevant).

– Can he delegate work to a third party? The ability to do so would indicate self-employment.

– What financial risk does he undertake – eg if the work is not completed on time, or not to an acceptable standard, does the person still get paid?

– Does he/she work for other clients and does not provide services exclusively to the charity?

If the person appears to satisfy these tests, and makes clear to the charity that he is self-employed, the charity should request written confirmation that they are paying their tax under Schedule D together with a note of their tax reference number. The charity should treat the individual as employed until this number is forthcoming. The individual is responsible for obtaining this number from his tax office.

If the worker is part-time then the same rules apply. Once it has been determined that the part-timer is an employee then he is treated no differently from other employees. Employees earning below the tax threshold should be asked to consider signing a form P46 certifying that this is their only employment. This form is then held by the employer in case of a visit by the Revenue.

Care needs to be taken with payments to volunteers. If these are specific payments for the provision of a service or reimbursement of an expense, there should not be a problem; but if they are regular payments for services which are similar to those provided by employees, it is likely that the person should be classed as an employee and the PAYE/NIC regulations imposed.

6.2.2 Emoluments

These include 'all salaries, fees, wages, perquisites and profits whatsoever'[1] from an office or employment. Emoluments do not just include only cash payments; 'benefits in kind' provided as a result of employment will also be

---

1   ICTA 1988, s 131(1).

included in emoluments, depending on the type of benefit and the total emoluments of the employee.

(1) What principles determine whether or not a payment or benefit is an emolument?

If entitlement to a payment is contractual, or provided for by the past or current practice of an employer, this is strong grounds for considering it to be an emolument. In *Moorhouse v Dooland*,[1] the taxpayer was a professional cricketer. Under the club rules, he was entitled to a bonus and a public collection whenever he played particularly well. In the 1951/52 season, he qualified on 11 occasions and received the proceeds of collections. The court held that the proceeds of the public collections were taxable on the grounds that they were a contractual right of the employee.

If the payment is made as a result of the office or employment, the identity of the payer is irrelevant. In *Blakiston v Cooper*,[2] a parish vicar received the customary Easter offering from the parishioners, and this was held to be taxable on the grounds that the payment was made in respect of the services he performed as parish priest. The fact that the payment was voluntary and not made by the employer was irrelevant. Also, the payments had occurred in the previous five years, so it was not a one-off instance.

Exceptionally, if the payment is made because of the personal qualities of the recipient, it may avoid tax. The facts of each case will determine whether the rule in *Moorhouse v Dooland* or the following rule should apply. In *Seymour v Reed*,[3] the taxpayer was again a professional cricketer, and in 1920 was granted entitlement to the proceeds of a public collection in his honour at one of the home matches. The benefit match was in the nature of a farewell to the player, and would not recur. This income was held not to be taxable on the grounds that it was not contractual and was more a gesture of appreciation. It was also of a non-recurring nature.

A similar case was *Moore v Griffiths*[4] where the footballer Bobby Moore received a payment from the Football Association in recognition of England's victory in the 1966 World Cup. This income was held not to be taxable because it was not contractual and was intended as a gesture of appreciation. It could be argued that this was of a non-recurring nature also, as the likelihood of its repetition is minimal.

It should be noted that payments to an employee for the performance of services beyond normal duties will also be treated as an emolument.

In the first of the cases cited, the emoluments were received from third parties, not from the employer; so who pays is irrelevant to the determination whether

1   (1955) 36 TC 1.
2   (1909) 5 TC 347.
3   (1927) 11 TC 625.
4   (1972) 48 TC 338.

the amount is taxable. However, there may be complications relating to who should account for the tax: the employer, the employee or the third party. Where payments are received by employees from third parties, the employer may, under certain circumstances, be required to deduct tax under PAYE. If the tax is not collectable by the employer under the PAYE regulations, the employee is responsible for payment of the tax.

(2)   *Benefits in kind*

As mentioned earlier, emoluments include the provision of non-monetary benefits. Some benefits are assessable on all employees, irrespective of their level of pay; others are taxable only on 'higher paid' employees, (meaning employees earning over £8,500 a year, including all expenses and benefits) and most directors, irrespective of their level of pay. This level of earnings has been maintained deliberately at the same point since 1979. Chancellor Nigel Lawson explained that the reason was to ensure that more or less everyone who received benefits would be taxed on them, rather than (as had originally been envisaged by Stafford Cripps) only truly highly-paid employees.

Where, however, the director has no 'material interest' in a company and it is non-profit making then the director's level of pay will be the determinant, not merely the fact that he or she is a director.

Benefits taxable and potentially liable to NIC for all employees include:

– mileage allowances to employees for using their own cars in excess of the 'fixed profit car scheme' rates now called Authorised Mileage Rates (AMR). If the mileage allowance paid exceeds the AMR, the employee can make a claim for business mileage based on the AMR and would only pay tax on the excess. There are individual schemes which have had specific Revenue approval and which do not exactly follow the general rules. For NIC purposes, the employer can also pay up to the AMR without incurring liability. Volunteer drivers may also receive AMR allowances tax free for organised voluntary work;

– lump sum payments to the employee for entertaining. By 'lump sum' is meant an allowance not specifically allocable to individual items of expenditure. The logic is that this is like an increase in salary, which could be spent on other items. Any parts of the lump sum allowance which are spent on bona fide entertaining for the charity can be claimed as tax deductible by the employee, but this will only be after tax has been paid under PAYE. Such payments are liable to Class 1 NIC unless they are specific and distinct contributions to business expenses;

– vouchers, including vouchers which can be converted into cash, transport warrants, credit tokens which can be exchanged for goods or services, vouchers securing entrance to an outside nursery, and entrance tickets are some of the types of taxable voucher. Luncheon vouchers to the value of a maximum of 15p per day (unchanged since 1978/1979) are tax-free; anything exceeding that is taxable. Most vouchers are liable to Class 1 NIC;

– accommodation provided as a result of employment. This need not necessarily be provided by the employer to be taxable on the employee. It is not taxable where it is necessary for the proper performance of the employee's duties that he should reside in such accommodation. The test is whether occupation of the particular premises, and no others, is essential to proper performance. It is also not taxable where the accommodation is provided for the better performance of the employee's duties and it is customary for employers to make such provision. Finally, it is not taxable where there are special security arrangements; this is the only rule of which directors can take advantage.

If the employee does not fit into one of these categories then he or she is taxable on the 'annual value' of the property irrespective of the salary level. The annual value means at present the gross rateable value under the old rating system. If the employee's emoluments are more than £8,500 then he or she will also be taxable on the provision by the employer of heating, lighting, cleaning, repairs, decoration, furniture and fittings. This applies even if the employee fits into one of the categories above and is not taxable on the value of the accommodation.

Broadly, taxable accommodation is subject to a Class 1A NIC charge where:

– council tax is paid by the employer. However, where an employer pays an employee's council tax when the employee has had to relocate and incur an additional council tax charge on an empty property, or when the employee has to leave temporarily his main residence but still has a council tax charge, it is unlikely that these payments by the employer will be taxable on the employee.[1] If the accommodation is necessary for the performance of the employee's duties there will also be no tax charge on the employee;
– relocation benefits are over £8,000. Expenses connected with buying and selling a home, moving possessions, temporary travel and preliminary visits qualify for inclusion in the exemption of £8,000. Expenses which do not qualify for exemption would be taxable. These include mortgage or housing subsidies if the employee moves to a higher cost area; interest payments for the present home; purchase of school uniforms; and compensation for loss on sale of present home.[2]

Relocation expenses which qualify for tax relief are generally not subject to NIC – there is no £8,000 limit.

(3) Higher paid employees' and directors' benefits
Benefits which are taxable only on employees whose emoluments exceed £8,500 include the following:

---

1   ICAEW Memorandum TR 795 and ESC A67.
2   See IR134 *Income tax and relocation packages* published October 1997.

- private use by the employee of a car owned by the employer. This is taxed by calculating 35%, or other percentage based on business mileage and age of the car, of the list price of the car and adding this to emoluments.[1] The cost of any improvements, including modifications necessary for disabled drivers, are not added to the list price and thus escape tax;
- car fuel made available to the employee in addition to a car, which is also used for private purposes, incurs a statutory scale charge added to emoluments, depending on the cubic capacity of the car's engine. If fuel is provided but the car is owned by the employee, the employee should be taxed on the cost of the fuel to the employer. There is a special lower charge of £500 where a van is made available to the employee for private use. This charge is £350 if the van is more than four years old;[2]
- loans to the employee where the interest rate is subsidised by the employer. The employee is taxed on the difference between the official interest rate, and the interest actually paid, subject to an exemption for loans of up to £5,000;
- the cost of private health insurance;
- a scholarship awarded by the employer, or another person connected to the employer, to a child of the employee, or to another member of the employee's family. The cost will be assessed as a benefit where it has been provided by reason of employment. In general terms, payments made by an employer for the purpose of training a current employee, or retraining an ex-employee, will not be assessable benefits where the training course is intended to impart technical skills to be used in the employment;
- assets provided for the use of the employee. There is an annual benefit equal to 20% of the market value of the asset when first made available, and the cost to the employer of the asset;
- an asset is given to the employee where the benefit is the greater of the cost of providing the asset and the market value of the asset in the employee's hands (the second-hand value);
- in-house facilities made available to the employee, where the general rule is that the employee is assessable on the marginal cost of the benefit. Marginal cost means the additional cost of making that benefit available to the employee, as for example, in *Pepper v Hart*,[3] where the children attended (at reduced fees) the school where their parents were teachers. The teachers were to be assessed on the extra cost of providing places for their children, which in this case was very little as there were surplus places. However, the provision of in-house sporting, social and recreational facilities are not assessable benefits;
- provision of cleaning, lighting, heating etc in relation to accommodation.

Specifically non-assessable benefits include approved pension provisions, contributions to the cost of a staff Christmas party as long as the total cost per

---

1   The rules concerning the taxation of company cars are in Sch 6 to ICTA 1988.
2   See Sch 6A to ICTA 1988 for the rules in relation to vans.
3   *Pepper v Hart* [1992] STC 898.

head is less than £75 and the provision of nursery care in the employer's crèches. However, the payment by the employer for places in other creches would be taxable.

(4) Termination payments

This is a complex area and our intention is to put the charity employer on notice that care and professional advice will be necessary in relation to termination payments. The general rule is that a payment received in connection with the termination of the holding of an office or employment, or any change in its functions or emoluments, whether made because of any legal obligation or not, is chargeable to tax under s 148 of ICTA 1988.

Lump sum payments are, therefore, not automatically exempt from normal tax rules. If the lump sum can be seen to relate to services already performed, it will be treated as an emolument and will be taxable in the normal way, not under the provisions of s 148. For example, this would be the case where a contract of employment provides for 12 months' employment at £300 per month and a lump sum of £6,400 at the cessation of the period of employment. Where the lump sum relates to services to be performed, it will also be taxed in the usual way, for example, where an employee agrees to accept £7,500 per year for the next five years in exchange for a lump sum of £8,000 now.

If a lump sum does not fall under s 148 the employee cannot take advantage of the 'golden handshake' provisions which state that payments made solely because of death or disability due to an accident will not be taxed at all. The first £30,000 of any other payments falling under s 148, such as for redundancy or loss of office, is tax-free. Statutory redundancy amounts are included in this figure.

Ex gratia ie non-contractual, payments do not necessarily fall under s 148. The Revenue feels that these should be treated as benefits under unapproved retirement benefits schemes, where the employee is retiring. Sections 647–648 of ICTA 1988, dealing with unapproved retirement schemes, therefore apply, which means that the £30,000 exemption does not apply. To the extent that a termination payment which is eligible for relief exceeds £30,000, that excess amount is taxable under PAYE as normal, treated as received on the date employment ceases.

6.2.3 National Insurance

'Employment' has substantially the same meaning for NIC purposes as for income tax purposes. Total NICs payable by self-employed people are considerably lower than those paid by employees. The differences between income tax and NIC arise over earnings.

Earnings for NIC purposes means gross pay before deducting any pension contributions, and without taking account of any deductions or reliefs which are allowable for income tax purposes. Gross pay means all emoluments paid in money, including any gratuities allocated by the employer, and any cash payments in lieu of a benefit in kind. Earnings formerly did not include the value of most benefits in kind (except cars) but, from April 2000, employer's NICs are exacted on most benefits in kind, except for beneficial loans and the provision of child-care. The employee will only pay NICs on earnings excluding benefits in kind except for vouchers and certain other special circumstances beyond the scope of this work.

Other items not included in earnings include any payments by way of a pension, redundancy payments and any contributions towards expenses actually incurred by the employee in the course of his employment.

There is a liability to NICs on the benefit of company cars but it is only payable by the employer (Class 1A). There is also a charge on fuel provided by the employer, again Class 1A. The position in relation to the reimbursement of employees for the use of their own cars is that NICs are chargeable on any excess over certain fixed mileage amounts as calculated in accordance with the income tax rules, detailed at **6.2.2(2)**.

6.2.4   IR35 – Personal services provided through intermediaries

From 6 April 2000, anti-avoidance legislation operates in the circumstances envisaged by the Chancellor, Gordon Brown:[1]

> 'There has for some time been general concern about the hiring of individuals through their own service companies so that they can exploit the fiscal advantages offered by a corporate structure. It is possible for someone to leave work on a Friday, only to return the following Monday to do exactly the same job as an indirectly engaged "consultant" paying substantially reduced tax and National Insurance.'

The legislation draws aside the corporate veil and taxes the individual concerned as if he was being paid emoluments by the organisation (the intermediary) of which he is a director. The onus here will be on the intermediary to test whether the legislation and, therefore, PAYE and NICs apply. The tests used to determine whether this is the case are those detailed earlier for determining whether or not an individual is employed or self-employed.

---

1   IR35 *Personal services provided through intermediaries* published 9 March 1999.

Chapter 7

LOCAL TAXATION AND CHARITIES

'Is it not a wonderful folly and cynicism which would throw on the hard-worked managers of charities the necessity of collecting hundreds or thousands a year beyond their past requirements, that the towns may have their rates reduced from 7s to 6s 11 ¾d in the £?'

William Lucas Sargant *Taxation: past, present, future.*

7.1   RATES AND CHARITIES

Of those taxes still in existence, the oldest we need to consider is rates, which remains with us in the form of the uniform business rate. As usual, some historical background may be useful when examining the relationship of rates with charities.

7.1.1   Historical background

During the period of the Catholic Church's ascendancy, from at least the Norman Conquest until the reformation of the monasteries in the 1530s, relief of the poor, health and education had been organised largely by the Church. When this ascendancy ceased, some of the finance and organisation of these three key social welfare activities remained with the Catholic Church's successor, the Church of England, but for the first time a significant amount passed into the control of secular trustees.[1] During Elizabeth I's reign, a material amount of the wealth of the nation became committed, via gifts and endowments, to charities linked to philanthropy in these areas of social welfare. Although the State was slowly increasing its involvement in relief of the poor, most of the effort fell on private philanthropy, manifested through charitable trusts, and religious bodies. As a historian[2] of the period says of the Tudor responses to the problem of the poor:

'The threats of slavery and branding in the Act of 1548 and of hanging in that of 1572 having failed to eradicate destitution and vagrancy, the state appealed to private charity; next it ordained that private charity should be stimulated by the moral suasion of the church and then by the sterner arguments of the justices of the peace; finding these ineffective, it authorised coercion and the levying of poor rates to be applied in providing work for the able-bodied poor and relief for the impotent poor.'

The Poor Relief Act 1601 was a development from two earlier Acts and provided the foundation for rating for the next 349 years. State involvement was to be

---

1   M Chesterman, *Charities, Trusts and Social Welfare* (Routledge, London, 1929).
2   AF Pollard, *The Political History of England Vol VI* (1910) pp 455–6.

exercised through the local authorities. The Act gave each parish the responsibility for the maintenance of its own poor by giving it powers of taxation, exercised by the overseers of the poor. In its early form therefore, it was a form of hypothecated taxation, with the connection between tax raised and expenditure of the tax immediately apparent. The Act was not specific about how the tax was to be raised. The overseers were required:[1]

> 'to raise ... by taxation of every inhabitant, parson, vicar and other and of every occupier of lands, houses, tithes impropriate or propriations of tithes, coal mines or saleable underwoods, in such competent sum or sums of money as they shall think fit ... for the relief of the poor.'

From early in the life of the tax, ability to pay became the basis for liability. *Sir Anthony Earby's Case* (2 Bulst 354) in 1633 established that assessments ought to be made according to the 'visible estate' of the inhabitants, both real and personal, and also that occupiers of land should be liable.

As the tax developed, the taxable unit of property became the 'hereditament', and personal property ceased to be assessed. Liability fell first on the occupier, but was supplemented by recourse to the owner to facilitate collection. The tax was levied at so much in the pound of the 'rateable value' of the hereditament. The amount per pound was known as the 'poundage', and was set by the local authority to take account of its budget for the forthcoming year. 'Rateable value' was, and is, a key concept of the rates; it was supposed to represent the annual letting value of the hereditament concerned, assuming the tenant had to maintain the property in its existing condition to command that rent. In short it was a hypothetical rent, but the assumptions behind its calculation varied widely.

The 1601 Act contained no exemption for property owned or occupied by charities, but the operation of the tax via the valuation of property made it possible for the taxing authorities to treat charities favourably by keeping the valuation of their property low. The contemporary view was that the burden for tending to the needs of the poor should fall upon private philanthropy and that the role of the local authority should be subordinate to this. It would have made little sense, therefore, to levy this tax on the very charities who were supposed to be carrying out much of this role. The logic was that if the charity was providing benefits for the community in which it was situated, eg providing poor relief, then this was keeping the poor rate lower than it would otherwise have been, and so the charity was entitled to favourable tax treatment for providing this service. Thus, the favourable treatment of a charity depended on the local rating authority setting the rateable value of charitable property at lower than its true value, or giving it no value at all.

By the end of the nineteenth century the situation was chaotic: charities in some areas had to pay relatively high rates, in others low rates, and in yet others no rates at all. However, the official legal position was that they were all liable.

---

1   Poor Relief Act 1601, s 1.

In 1893, there was a case which established that absence of a profit-making motive was no ground for exemption from the rates – *LCC v Erith Parish (Churchwardens) and Dartford Union Assessment Committee* [1893] AC 562.

The position of charity property can be contrasted with some types of property which were exempt from rates. These included Crown property; places of religious worship; Sunday schools and ragged schools; and property occupied by literary and scientific societies. Crown property was exempt by virtue of the fact that it was not mentioned as being potentially taxable in the Act of 1601; places of religious worship were exempted by the Poor Rate Exemption Act 1833; ragged schools and Sunday schools by the Exemption from Rating Act 1869; and literary and scientific societies by the Scientific Societies Act 1843.

7.1.2 Twentieth-century reforms

This unevenness in the calculation of rateable value led to demands for standardisation. Some charities in higher rated areas, such as the rapidly developing urban centres, felt that the system was discriminatory. The large urban voluntary hospitals felt this in particular, because of the increasing financial pressure to which they were exposed due to their position as the main source of health care for the urban masses. An attempt was made at the standardisation of rateable values with the Rating and Valuation Act 1925, but wide variations in the valuation of charity land continued.

A more serious attempt at standardisation was made in 1948, by which time the voluntary hospitals were being absorbed into the new National Health Service and were thus leaving the charity sector. The Local Government Act 1948 transferred the responsibility for valuing land for rateable purposes from the local rating authorities to the Inland Revenue – a move which was expected to impose standard valuation procedures. This would have led directly to the removal of the sympathetic under-valuation of charitable property. It was recognised, however, that to impose full liability for rates on all charities would have caused substantial hardship to many of those who had relied for many years on the sympathy of their local authority. Instead, a complex compromise was reached whereby charities continued to enjoy the same proportion of rate relief they had received from under-valuation.

This over-complex system soon generated criticism and the Pritchard committee[1] was appointed to review it. The committee's report in 1959 recommended that all charitable organisations should be entitled to claim mandatory relief of 50% of the rates chargeable on land and premises occupied by them, as long as the premises were used wholly or mainly for charitable purposes. It also recommended that charities should have the right to ask the local authority, in its discretion, for relief against the remaining 50%. These recommendations became law in the Rating and Valuation Act 1961 and were

---

1   Report of the Committee on the Rating of Charities and Kindred Bodies, Cmnd 831, *Parliamentary Papers 1958/59* Vol 19.

re-enacted in subsequent legislation. Valuation would now be standardised, with charities having a specific statutory exemption, though this was partly discretionary. The previous exemptions for places of public religious worship and certain types of schools were continued. The relevant wording of the legislation initiating the exemption was as follows:

> 'If notice in writing is given to the rating authority that:
>
>   (a)   any hereditament occupied by, or by trustees for, a charity and wholly or
>   mainly used for charitable purposes (whether of that charity or of that
>   and other charities); or
>
>   (b)   any other hereditament, being a hereditament held upon trust for use as
>   an almshouse
>
> ... then ... the amount of any rates shall not exceed one half ...'[1]

This favourable tax treatment of charities regarding local tax was made available to all legally recognised charities, whether national or local. The informal requirement that charities should provide benefit to the community in which they were based, which had been the foundation for the old favourable treatment of charities for local taxation, was no longer considered to be relevant: charitable status was sufficient. This represented an extension of charitable exemption.

There were problem areas though, as always with fiscal law in contact with the real world, and the interpretation of the phrase 'wholly or mainly used for charitable purposes' became the subject of some contention. In *Glasgow Corporation v Johnstone*,[2] Lord Reid stated:

> 'If the use which the charity makes of the premises is directly to facilitate the
> carrying on of its main charitable purposes that is, in my view, sufficient to satisfy
> the requirement that the premises are used for charitable purposes.'

This view was restricted by a case involving the rating position of premises used by a charity for fund raising. In *Oxfam v City of Birmingham*,[3] the House of Lords held that charity shops run by Oxfam were not 'wholly or mainly used for charitable purposes', rather they were used for the raising of funds, which funds would then be used for the purposes of the charity proper. This decision provoked a legislative response: the 1967 Act was amended in 1976 to except charity shops from the general rule that premises should be used for charitable purposes only, if they were to be eligible for the exemption. The legislation as it stands now is as follows:

> 'A hereditament shall be treated as wholly or mainly used for charitable purposes at
> any time if at the time it is wholly or mainly used for the sale of goods donated to a
> charity and the proceeds of the sale of the goods (after any deduction of expenses)
> are applied for the purposes of a charity.'[4]

---

1   Rating and Valuation Act 1961, s 11 now re-enacted as LGFA 1988, s 47.
2   [1965] AC 609.
3   [1975] 2 All ER 289.
4   LGFA 1988, s 64(10).

The definition of charity shop for this purpose was held to be a shop where it can be shown that all or most of the goods sold have been donated by the public. If the charity shop is selling bought-in goods, this can endanger the eligibility, and the general rule that charity shops and premises used for fundraising are taxable, still holds. One curiosity is that the head office of a charity has been held to be used wholly or mainly for charitable purposes, on the basis that the charity could not function without it. The device whereby charities are allowed to put their fund-raising activities into trading companies, and then passes the profits tax-free back to the charity, has no counterpart in rates law.

Local taxation was the subject of considerable political interest during the 1980s and the law governing rates is now found in LGFA 1988 and LGFA 1992. The tax base for local taxation is now split between uniform business rate (UBR), levied on property occupied for non-domestic purposes; and council tax, which is assessed on dwellings. The philosophy behind the 1988 legislation was to remove the power of local authorities to set the level of rates. So a tax which had originally given local authorities the power to determine their own tax level was henceforward only to be collected by those authorities, not set by them.

Post-1988, the amount payable is calculated in a fashion similar to that used before, but using a 'multiplier' rather than poundage against rateable value. This 'multiplier' is set by the Government, and applies over the whole country, hence the term 'uniform'. Rates therefore continue to be potentially charge-able on all land and buildings which are not domestic, so the word 'business' is misleading. The 50% exemption has now been extended to 80%, and the remaining 20% is subject to a further discretionary exemption. The rules about 'wholly or mainly used' etc still hold. The discretion to exempt a charity totally from rates lies with the local authority. It has been suggested[1] that the following questions might be asked by a local authority in determining whether it should exercise its discretion, with positive answers weighing in favour of exemption.

- Is membership of the organisation open to the whole community? Are there no barriers to membership? If so, are the barriers reasonable?
- Is the catchment area for the organisation's membership predomi-nantly within the local authority area?
- Is there active encouragement of membership from sections of the community which the authority considers particularly deserving?
- Can a wider section of the community than just the members use the organisation's facilities?
- Has the organisation exercised self-help in the construction and maintenance of facilities?

---

1   W J McClusky and P J Moss *The Uniform Business Rate* (Tolleys, 1992) p 109.

A further reason for exercising the discretionary power to reduce or cancel the rates bill of a charity is where, in the authority's view, the charging of rates would sustain hardship, and it would be reasonable to cancel the charge. The definition of 'hardship' was raised in *R v Liverpool City Council, ex parte Windsor Securities Ltd.*[1]

Unoccupied property owned by a charity can qualify for exemption if it can be seen that when it is next in use the occupation will be wholly or mainly for charitable purposes. Other unoccupied property is chargeable at 50% of the full rates.

7.1.3   Conclusion

To conclude, rates can constitute a considerable charge for charities. The 1994 report[2] of the task force set up to reduce bureaucracy in the sector expressed charities' concern in relation to discretionary relief not being made available to charities which do not need to be registered with the Charities Commission; and the valuation of certain charitable properties, such as village halls. The main demand was for the removal of the discretionary element of relief. This was rejected by the government of the time.

7.2   COUNCIL TAX AND CHARITIES

This tax was introduced by LGFA 1992 to replace the disastrous community charge, or poll tax. It continues, albeit in a circumscribed fashion, the tradition of local authorities having some power over the level of taxation they set; a tradition now ended for the rates. It is payable on all dwellings except exempt dwellings, and is the counterpart of UBR, which taxes non-domestic property (or property which is not a dwelling). It contains no exemptions for charities as such: they have no special treatment, but can take advantage of the general exemptions as they become relevant.

The liability for council tax falls primarily on the occupier of the dwelling, but if there is no occupier, the owner is liable. The charging authority can decide to charge the owner rather the occupier in the case of:

- residential care homes, nursing homes or hostels;
- dwellings inhabited by religious communities;
- homes in multiple occupation, such as houses divided into student flats.

The likeliest situation where charities would become liable for council tax would be when a charity owns any of these types of property. Certain types of property are exempted from a council tax charge because they are unoccupied

---

1   (1979) RA 159 (CA).
2   Charities and Voluntary Organisations Task Force Proposals, July 1994.

for specific reasons. Unoccupied property is not exempt, but subject to a 50% council tax charge. Exempt dwellings for council tax purposes include the following:

– vacant dwellings needing structural renewal to make them habitable;
– dwellings owned by a charity and unoccupied for less than 6 months;
– dwellings which are the homes of people resident elsewhere for the purposes of their studies;
– dwellings which are being kept for occupation by ministers of religion;
– dwellings unoccupied because the occupier is living or detained elsewhere due to being in prison or mental care;
– dwellings unoccupied because the occupier is in hospital, nursing home or residential care;
– dwelling unoccupied because the occupier is resident elsewhere to take care of others;
– student halls of residence.

7.2.1 How is the liability calculated?

The local authority calculates a standard tax charge, based on projected budgeted expenditure and estimated sources of finance from elsewhere. This charge is applied to the taxpayers of the area via the valuation of dwellings.

The valuation for council tax is different from that used for rates purposes. It is based on the open market value of the dwelling, which means as if sold on the open market by a willing vendor on 1 April 1991. The council tax valuation is a capital valuation, whereas the rateable value was a revenue value, ie an estimate of annual income from the property. Special fixtures in a disabled person's home are ignored for valuation purposes if they increase the value of the dwelling, but are taken into account if they reduce the value.

The council tax valuations are banded. The standard charge referred to earlier is set in relation to valuation band D and then apportioned to other bands. The purpose behind the banding is that once the position of a dwelling within a band has been set, no more revaluations should be necessary because the relative values between dwellings will not change, unless the property changes its nature. So the political furore which always attended revaluations under the old rates system should not occur.

The bands for England currently are:

A	Up to £40,000	E	£88,001–120,000
B	£40,001–52,000	F	£120,001–160,000
C	£52,001–68,000	G	£160,001–320,000
D	£68,001–88,000	H	£320,001 +

There is a right of appeal against the valuation of a dwelling.

The basic charge for council tax assumes that there are two or more adults in occupation in the dwelling. The charge will be reduced if there are fewer, as follows:

Single occupation   25% discount
Unoccupied   50% discount, such as second homes, or where all
                                        occupants fall into categories listed below.

In counting the number of adults in occupation, the following are not included:

- full-time students;
- those in hospital or care, or severely mentally impaired;
- those in hostels or night shelters;
- careworkers, defined as a person engaged in providing care or support to another person on behalf of a charity or local authority. The carer must be employed by the charity or local authority and reside in the dwelling;
- members of religious communities, such as monks and nuns;
- certain international visitors, eg soldiers; and
- those in prison, meaning that the charge for the dwelling which is the sole or main residence of the prisoner will be reduced accordingly.

For example, a dwelling which contains a severely mentally impaired person and a carer will have its council tax reduced to 50%, just as if it were unoccupied. Liability for the tax may accrue to a person who is a non-person in terms of numbers of inhabitants; for example, a person in prison who is an owner-occupier will be liable for the council tax when he is released.

The establishment of council tax brought an end to the upheavals in local taxation that had marked the 1980s. It has bedded down very well and its continued existence is not in question.

Chapter 8

TAXATION OF DISASTER FUNDS AND CHARITY LOTTERIES

*'Destruction upon destruction is cried; for the whole land is spoiled:
suddenly are my tents spoiled, and my curtains in a moment.'*

Jeremiah 4.20

8.1 TAXATION OF DISASTER FUNDS

A disaster fund is an appeal for donations in response to a one-off disaster, as opposed to attempts to address a long-standing and continuing perceived need. When donations are received in response to a disaster, the danger is that the fund set up to gather and use the donations will not receive charitable status. An appeal for funds is often launched immediately with great publicity and the money starts to flood in; indeed, often the money starts to arrive before any trust deed is drawn up. The organisers of the appeal will usually want to give as much as possible to the victims of the disaster.

At this stage, the organisers need to make some decisions before they start handing out money. The appeal can only be considered charitable if it is purely for the relief of need. Amounts given over and above this level of need may jeopardise the granting of charitable status with a consequent absence of tax relief. Valuable tax reliefs may otherwise be available, as we have seen in previous chapters, to both donors and the fund. The organisers therefore need to decide whether the fund is to be charitable, or whether a more flexible fund structure should be established, with a mixture of charitable and non-charitable funds.

Where the organisers want a charitable fund, they should ensure that the trust deed states that surplus funds will be utilised for another charitable purpose. Official guidance in this area is available (prompted by the failure of the Penlee lifeboat disaster fund to achieve charitable status in 1982), in the form of the Guidelines on Disaster Appeals issued by the Attorney-General. Also, the Inland Revenue and Customs and Excise issued joint Guidelines on the Tax Treatment of Disaster Funds in 1989, which was updated in February 1994 (FRP 6/68). The discussion which follows combines the gist of each of these documents.

8.1.1 What are the pros and cons of different types of appeal?

Charitable funds attract generous direct tax reliefs but cannot be used to give individual benefits over and above those appropriate to their needs. Also, the operation of a charitable fund will be subject to the scrutiny of the Charity Commissioners.

As noted in Chapter 4, the funds from events such as concerts, galas, football matches, record releases (including copyright royalties), publications, etc are free of direct tax (by ESC4) for a charitable organisation. Such one-off events, if held by a charity, a company owned by a charity, or by bodies of a political, religious or philosophical nature, are eligible for exemption from VAT.[1]

Non-charitable funds attract no particular tax reliefs, and donations to them do not receive special tax treatment, but under a non-charitable trust there is no limit on the amount which can be paid to individual beneficiaries. Also, there will be no scrutiny by the Charity Commissioners. For the type of one-off events mentioned earlier, all receipts will normally be taxable, but where a basic minimum charge is set, any additional free-will donations will not count towards taxable profits if they are:

– given by persons attending the event; and
– collected on behalf of, and passed on to, the trustees of the non-charitable trust.

This concession is not available for trading events organised by a company, whether or not part of that company's existing trade, and the proceeds of the fundraising event will initially be taxed on the company. There is a way of avoiding corporation tax on the net proceeds, however, by paying over to the charity via the Gift Aid provisions.

One-off events organised by a non-charitable entity (unless it is wholly owned by a charity) will not be eligible for exemption of income, so such income will be standard-rated for VAT purposes, apart from that amount which qualifies as a donation. Input tax on attributable costs will be recoverable in the normal way.

With non-charitable appeals, particular care should be taken to ensure:

– that there is no doubt who is to benefit;
– whether or not this benefit is at the discretion of the trustees;
– whether or not the entire benefit of the appeal is to go to the beneficiaries;
– if not, what will happen to the surplus funds, otherwise the trust may fail for uncertainty, and the surplus funds may have to be returned to the donors, with all the expense this would entail.

The Joint Statement[2] suggests that a practical solution at the start of the disaster fund is to establish two parallel trusts: a discretionary charitable trust, and a non-charitable discretionary trust. It is suggested that it is desirable to receive and hold the bulk of donations in the non-charitable fund, because this gives the trustees freedom to distribute funds in accordance with donors' wishes.

---

1   See Chapter 10 for details of the VAT rules for exemption of one-off events.
2   FRP6/68.

This advice was pre-Gift Aid, though the point still holds, as not many people are likely to donate more than £250 to a disaster appeal.

The trustees of the non-charitable trust should have the power to transfer income or other funds to the charitable trust. This will allow the charitable trust to recover the tax suffered by the trustees where it might not otherwise be recoverable by individual beneficiaries. The trustees of the charitable trust should also have the power to receive donations directly, for the following reasons:

– donations could be directed to this trust to take advantage of Gift Aid, and the capital tax exemptions (CGT and IHT). Also, corporate donations should be made to this trust;
– if other charities are contributing, they should do it to this trust, otherwise it may not be a charitable use of their funds.

Payments which can properly be considered to be for charitable purposes (such as the relief of poverty) can be first met from this charitable fund. It is suggested that this parallel structure would give flexibility, and as it has been proposed by the Revenue, it should be watertight.

8.2   TAXATION OF CHARITY LOTTERIES

Noting the chronic British tendency to gamble, charities frequently resort to the devising of games of chance to entice funds from the British public. A major device is the lottery, where tickets are sold on the chance of a prize. Charities who operate lotteries would formerly have had to consider the conditions for exemption from income and corporation tax in ESC C4, which are discussed in Chapter 4. If the lottery became a regular and significant activity, the surpluses generated would be taxed as trading and income and corporation tax could be payable. Because of this, a lottery would escape tax if run through a trading subsidiary. However, surpluses from lotteries are specifically exempted from income and corporation tax by s 505(1)(f) of ICTA 1988, as long as the lottery is in accordance with the Lotteries and Amusements Act 1976.

In terms of VAT, lotteries may be business or non-business depending on their scale and regularity. Where it is a business activity the granting of a right to take part in a lottery is exempt from VAT under VATA 1994 Sch 9, Group 4. Business or non-business treatment therefore makes little practical difference to the VAT position.[1] Other forms of betting will also be subject to the requirements of ESC C4, but some of them also have their own taxation regimes. These are contained in the Betting and Gaming Duties Act 1981; the duties being collected by Customs and Excise. Anyone promoting games of chance,

---

1   Home Office *Charities and Voluntary Organisations Task Force Proposals for Reform*, Full Report (The Stationery Office, 1994) p 28 (Customs' response to a recommendation).

competitions, raffles etc, should seek a ruling from Customs before the event goes ahead to ensure that it is treated correctly and no penalties are incurred.

Bingo duty is one of the duties in the Act and it is reasonably obvious what this charges, but if the proceeds of the bingo session are not for private gain, no bingo duty is payable. Charities operating bingo events therefore need not pay bingo duty, though once again clearance should be sought. Similarly, no gaming machine licence duty is payable if the proceeds from the machines are not for private gain. Lastly, no pool betting duty is payable if the benefits of the pool betting accrue to a charity.

Although not strictly a subject directly concerned with taxation, it is appropriate here to mention the National Lottery, which started in November 1994, because a national lottery is, in a sense, a form of voluntary taxation. When this Lottery began, opinion within the sector was divided about the benefits it would bring. Some felt that it would bring about a reduction in charitable donations because sums which would have been donated to charity would now be spent on the Lottery. Research has not supported this view. It is certain that thousands of charities have applied for and received funding from the Lottery; funding they would never otherwise have received.

Chapter 9

CONCEPTS OF VALUE ADDED TAX (VAT)

'A simple tax'

An early promise

9.1 INTRODUCTION

This chapter's main purpose is to examine the concepts of VAT, before looking at the complexities of how charities are affected by VAT. It is important, at the beginning, to understand that there is no general exemption from VAT for charitable organisations. VAT law does not contain the detailed but wide-ranging exemptions granted in favour of charities in income tax, CGT, and IHT legislation. There is no alternative but to explore and comprehend VAT vocabulary before we can assess how VAT rules deal with charities.

9.2 BACKGROUND

The conceptual basis of VAT was first developed by a German businessman and government adviser named Wilhelm von Siemens, who suggested that his proposals be introduced in Germany after the First World War. Siemens' proposals were stimulated by the inadequacies of the existing turnover taxes in Germany, but were never put into practice. The first real attempt to put a value added tax into practice in recognisable form was the French introduction of TVA[1] in 1954. This was also an attempt to deal with the inadequacies of existing turnover taxes and was on a limited scale. Its subsequent development in France was to provide the model which was adopted by the EC as a common system of tax for the development of a common market in goods and services across the Community. The appeal of the tax lies in its theoretical elegance and apparent simplicity, in its cheapness in collection, in the difficulty in evasion and lack of loop-holes for avoidance.

In Britain, the rate of VAT more than doubled between 1979 and 1995 and the base of the tax was extended by reducing the scope of zero rating. The rationale behind this was that direct tax reduces the citizen's freedom of choice by taking the tax away before any spending decisions can be made. VAT on the other hand is only paid when a spending decision is made by the citizen. Many of the essentials of life have been covered by zero-rating in the UK, thus making them

---

1   TVA stands for Taxe sur la Valeur ajoutée and was given its name by Maurice Lauré, Inspecteur des Finances at the time.

effectively free of VAT. As zero-rating is whittled away, in accordance with the EC's wishes, the effect of VAT on the UK economy has been very damaging.[1] Furthermore, VAT is a regressive tax, meaning that it forms a higher proportion of the poor's expenditure than that of the rich. It therefore hits the poor harder, and this will be exacerbated by the extension of the VAT base into the essentials of life, like fuel, food and travel.

The statutory philosophy of VAT is different from the taxes we have considered so far, since it originates in EU law. The statute passed by the UK Parliament, which introduced VAT, was the implementation of the EU 1st and 2nd Directives. The Directive most directly related to the form and structure of VAT is the 6th Directive, originally passed in 1977 and substantially amended in 1991.[2] In cases where there is a conflict between UK and EU law in relation to VAT, EU law takes priority. There is, however, a rule that where domestic law is in conflict with the EU law, Customs cannot rely on EU law to the detriment of the registered trader.

The statute imposing VAT is comparatively succinct – compare the size of VATA 1994 to ICTA 1988 – because VAT is initiated by general provisions, which are then embellished by statutory instruments or VAT leaflets. This, in practice, makes it a very fragmented tax, with a vast array of specific orders, and therefore more difficult for the layperson to comprehend. It is easy, though, to see the appeal of VAT to a government with a heavy legislative programme: statutory instruments and VAT leaflets can be introduced away from the direct scrutiny of Parliament.

Although compared to other taxes VAT is new in the UK, having been introduced by FA 1972, it has already gathered a considerable amount of case law, in the form of VAT tribunal rulings and higher court decisions. In addition, EU legislation and tax appeals may have direct effect in Member States. If Parliament has failed to implement an EU provision, the taxpayer can rely upon direct effect in the UK courts. Taking all this into account, it is not surprising that that early promise of simplicity has not been borne out by the reality of VAT.

9.3   THE SCOPE OF VAT

It is necessary to explore some of the key terms in the vocabulary of VAT, and then attempt to see how the tax is supposed to operate. The main charging provision of VATA 1994 is s 4, entitled 'Scope of tax', which states:

---

1   See Chapter 11 for further discussion of European developments.
2   The original 6th Directive's official reference is 77/388/EEC, and the 1991 amendments 91/680/EEC.

'(1) VAT shall be charged on any supply of goods and services made in the
      UK where it is a taxable supply made by a taxable person in the course or
      furtherance of any business carried on by him.
(2) A taxable supply is a supply of goods and services made in the UK other
      than an exempt supply.'

VAT is not a tax on profits, it is essentially a tax on transactions, eg sales, which is
ultimately borne by the final consumer, at least in theory. The actual
distribution of the tax burden differs from this where there are anomalies in
the types of supply made by organisations, as we shall see with charities, and this
can mean that the effective incidence of the tax often stops short of the final
consumer.

The following component terms can be extracted from s 4:

–   taxable supply of goods;
–   taxable supply of services;
–   taxable person;

In the course or furtherance of business.

9.3.1   Taxable supply of goods and services

VAT is a tax levied on turnover. This is calculated on the value, actual or
deemed, of the supply of goods and services (known as 'taxable supplies'),
which are supplied by the registered taxpayer. Taxable supplies are supplies of
all types of goods and services other than those that fall within the exemptions
contained in Sch 9 to VATA 1994.

What is meant by 'supply'? A transfer of the whole property in goods is a supply
of goods, but there can be a supply when the transfer is of stolen goods, ie where
the vendor has no good title. There can be supplies in tax terms when no
consideration is present, at least of goods; for example, when an employer gives
a Christmas hamper to an employee. The statute does not contain a definition
of supply but HM Customs and Excise publication *The General Guide to VAT*
(VAT Notice 700) at p 6 explains that:

> 'You supply goods if you pass the exclusive ownership of goods to another person.
> You supply services if you do something, other than supplying goods, for a
> consideration. A consideration is any form of payment in money or in kind,
> including anything which is itself a supply.'

Thus, all supplies are potentially taxable but the liability to account for the tax
arises only when the supply is made by a taxable person in the course of a
business carried on by him. Supplies are exempt only if they are specifically
exempted by law. Supplies are outside the scope of the tax if they are made by
someone who is not a taxable person, or made outside the UK (subject to some
exceptions), or not made in the course or furtherance of business.

9.3.2   Taxable person

A taxable person is someone who makes or intends to make taxable supplies and who is either registered or required to be registered. The definition therefore really concerns registration requirements, which are mandatory. An organisation is required to register for VAT if its taxable income is above the annual threshold (currently £52,000). Business income, for these purposes, is defined as income relating to an activity that is concerned with making supplies for a consideration, has a degree of frequency and is continued over a reasonable period of time.[1]

Registration can be achieved voluntarily if HM Customs and Excise are satisfied that taxable supplies are being made. Exempt supplies are not taxable supplies. An organisation making only exempt supplies cannot register for VAT, and neither can an organisation making only supplies which are outside the scope of VAT.[2]

9.3.3   In the course or furtherance of business

This phrase has created a considerable body of case-law as it is not defined in the legislation. 'Business' has a wider meaning for VAT than the income tax terms 'trade, profession or vocation'. There is no requirement of profit motive.

A leading case is *HM Customs and Excise Commrs v Morrison's Academy Boarding Houses Association.*[3] This concerned an association set up to provide accommodation for the pupils of a Scottish school. The association charged fees for this service but there was no profit motive present. The view of Lord Emslie was:

> 'In my opinion it will never be possible or desirable to define exhaustively "business" ... What one must do, is to discover what are the activities of the taxable person in course of which taxable supplies are made. If these activites are, as in this case, predominantly concerned with the making of taxable supplies to consumers for a consideration, it seems to me to ... enable one to conclude that the taxable person is in the "business of making taxable supplies ..." Further I can see no possible justification for the necessity of there being any "commercial" element in these activities to bring the association's supplies within the scope of the tax.'

The decision in this case was subsequently reinforced by a case involving a landowner, who arranged shooting parties on his land for his friends, but asked for a contribution towards the costs: *HM Customs and Excise Commrs v Lord*

---

1   The Customs view of the legal status of the various leaflets they produce giving advice and interpretation on VAT is:
> 'Generally speaking, this Notice and the other VAT notices and leaflets explain how Customs and Excise interpret the VAT law. However, sometimes the law says that the detailed rules on a particular matter will be set out in a notice or leaflet published by Customs rather than in a statutory instrument. When this is done that part of the notice or leaflet has legal force; and that fact will be clearly shown at the relevant point in the publication.'
2   See further VAT Notice 700/1 – 'Should I be registered for VAT?'.
3   [1978] STC 1.

Fisher.[1] Customs sought to establish that these contributions were taxable supplies made in the course of business. The taxpayer was already registered for other activities in relation to his estate. The following tests were identified:

- Is the activity a serious undertaking earnestly pursued, or alternatively, a serious occupation not necessarily confined to a commercial or profit making undertaking?
- Is the activity an occupation or function actively pursued with reasonable or recognisable continuity?
- Does the activity have a certain measure of substance as measured by the value of taxable supplies made?
- Is the activity conducted in a regular manner and on sound and recognised business principles?
- Is the activity predominantly concerned with the making of taxable supplies to consumers for a consideration?
- Are the taxable supplies of a kind which are commonly made by those who seek to profit by them?

Positive answers would point towards the activity being seen as a business. The taxable supply must be made in the course or furtherance of a business, and this means that activities which would not normally be thought of as falling in the normal course of business may be taxable. HM Customs and Excise lost the case on the following grounds:

> 'What Lord Fisher did was to arrange shooting for pleasure and social enjoyment. In our judgement this constitutes a non-business activity. Furthermore ... the fact that those concerned made contributions to the expenses did not have the effect of turning what is essentially a non-business activity into a business.'[2]

Another earlier case, *HM Customs and Excise Commrs v Royal Exchange Theatre Trust*,[3] which set some limit on the wide-ranging definition of business, involved a trust set up to convert the Manchester Cotton Exchange into a theatre. A charitable trust was established to convert the premises and construct the theatre, being financed by various fundraising campaigns, and the trust then handed over the theatre for zero consideration to a separate charitable company. The trust had made no taxable supplies. The case revolved around whether the activities of raising funds and constructing the theatre amounted to a business for VAT purposes. If so, VAT incurred on purchases would have been recoverable. The trust was unsuccessful:

> 'The trustees no doubt carried on their affairs with great skill and in a "business-like" manner. But so might a private philanthropist. Looking at the activities of these trustees as a whole it seems to me that they lacked any commercial element at all and that they cannot properly be regarded as business activities.'

---

1   [1981] STC 238.
2   [1981] STC 238.
3   [1979] STC 728.

Another case, decided along similar lines, was *Greater London Red Cross Blood Transfusion Service v HM Customs and Excise Commrs.*[1] The Service is a charitable organisation whose object is to provide a blood transfusion service, and whose members are the volunteer donors who attend to give their blood. The charity charged a fee to hospitals to cover administrative costs and the case was about whether these fees were taxable.

> 'In our view, in this appeal ... we have to ask ourselves whether the activities of the Service do amount to a business, giving that word the wide meaning indicated as appropriate in the authorities above, or amount to no more than a part of a voluntary service to the community. If we, the members of this tribunal, regularly attended at a hospital to give our blood, we do not consider that, individually, we could be justifiably accused of giving our blood in the course or furtherance of a business carried on by us. Further, we do not consider the receipt only of travelling expenses by such a donor converts the activity into a business. Basically, the activity still remains, in our view, a voluntary service to the community notwithstanding the payment of such expenses. [This case] exemplifies the distinction between a business for tax purposes and a voluntary service to the community, which we consider to be a valid and relevant distinction ...'

9.4   THE OPERATION OF VAT

To see how VAT operates, we need to explore the application of certain terms:

- output tax;
- input tax;
- standard rate;
- zero rate;
- exempt; and
- outside the scope.

VAT is an indirect tax because it is collected by intermediaries. The real cost of the tax falls on the final consumer, but the tax is collected before the final consumer gets his hands on the goods. The tax is collected at each stage where value is added. In effect this means each stage in the business chain. VAT Notice 700 devotes a small but succinct section to 'How VAT works':

> 'If you make standard-rated supplies, you have to account to Customs and Excise for the tax due. This is your output tax. Normally, you charge the tax to your customers. If your customers are registered for VAT and the supplies are for use in their business, the tax is their input tax. In the same way tax charged to you on your business purchases is your input tax.
>
> As a registered person, you can reclaim from Customs and Excise as much of the VAT on your purchases, and imports, as relates to the standard-rated and zero-rated supplies you make. In principle, you cannot reclaim VAT which relates to any non-business activity or to any exempt supplies you make.

---

1   [1983] VATTR 241.

At predetermined intervals you pay to Customs and Excise the excess of your output tax over the VAT you reclaim as input tax. If the input tax you can reclaim is more than your output tax, you can reclaim the difference from Customs and Excise.'[1]

The situation remains simple where the outputs of a business are wholly standard-rated but to illuminate a typical charity's position we need to consider zero-rating, exempt supplies and outside the scope activities.

9.4.1 Zero-rating

There are three rates of VAT in the UK: 17.5%, 5% and 0%. Zero rate was introduced and is retained for social and political reasons, although its future is under threat.[2] The zero-rated supplies are listed in Sch 8 to VATA 1994. When supplies are zero-rated, the supplier is entitled to register and, even though no VAT is charged on supplies made, the supplier is able to recover any input suffered. Certain businesses thus become recipients of funds from HM Customs and Excise, such as shipping companies.[3]

9.4.2 Exempt supplies

By contrast with zero-rating, an organisation which makes exempt supplies only, or supplies outside the scope of VAT, cannot levy output VAT on its supplies. Because it has no taxable supplies, it has no tax against which to set any input tax it suffers. This input tax therefore becomes a cost to the organisation, rather than being passed on down the commercial chain. The list of exempt supplies is contained in Sch 9 to VATA 1994.

9.4.3 Outside the scope

Activities which are non-business activities are outside the scope of VAT. They do not generate transactions which enter into calculations for VAT purposes. Thus, any VAT incurred on purchases which are to be used for activities outside the scope is not input VAT and cannot feature in any partial exemption calculation. Such activities do not generate 'supplies' in any shape or form. Examples are donations, and dividends from shareholdings.

9.4.4 Partial exemption

What happens when an organisation has a mixture of supplies: some standard; some exempt or outside the scope? How much of the VAT incurred on purchases by that organisation can be set against output VAT? In this situation, there are various different types of VAT on purchases:

(1) exclusively attributable to exempt supplies;

---

1   VAT Notice 700 *The General Guide to VAT*, p 5.
2   See Chapter 11.
3   VATA 1994, Sch 8, Group 8.

(2)   exclusively attributable to outside the scope activities;

(3)   exclusively attributable to standard-rated supplies;

(4)   exclusively attributable to zero-rated supplies;

(5)   not attributable to any particular type of supply, eg on overheads.

How is each type to be treated? In particular, how much of each can be deducted from the organisation's output VAT.

Type (1) cannot be deducted from output tax, except where it, together with an appropriate percentage of non-attributable costs (type 5), does not exceed £625 per month on average (as revealed by a calculation at the end of the year); and VAT incurred on exempt supplies must not be more that 50% of the VAT on all purchases.

Type (2) is not input tax at all and can never be deducted from output tax.

Type (3) can be deducted in full from output tax.

Type (4) can be reclaimed in full from Customs.

Type (5) is the problem area, where special rules are in place to determine how much is reclaimable. Customs has what it calls the 'standard method' of calculation, which should be used in the absence of any special arrangement between the organisation and Customs. However, it is always worthwhile trying to come up with a method of calculation which is as favourable as possible to the organisation, although such non-standard methods cannot be used until Customs' approval is received. Such methods might include the attribution of VAT on the basis of numbers of employees engaged in different activities, some of which are exempt etc. This is discussed further in Chapter 10.

9.5   PENALTIES

No introduction to VAT regulation would be complete without an overview of the penalties imposed when errors are made. VAT is an unforgiving tax when it comes to innocent error. The system, as revised by FA 1985, was subsequently consolidated into VATA 1994. Penalties will be imposed, where required, in addition to the unpaid tax. These penalties can be summarised as follows:

9.5.1   Late returns – s 59

If a VAT return is not received on time, and there is an amount due to Customs, a default surcharge will be imposed. The amount of the surcharge depends on the number of times it has occurred before, reaching a maximum of 15% of the outstanding tax. If the payment is received on time but the return is late, a default is registered but the rate of surcharge, which will normally increase with each default, will not increase.

9.5.2   Tax evasion – s 60(1)

Tax evasion, ie, dishonestly under-paying tax or claiming refunds, will produce a penalty of the amount of the tax evaded or claimed, whether or not the case involves criminal liability.

9.5.3   Incorrect certificate – s 60(2) and (3)

Where a person, such as a charity, gives a certificate to a supplier incorrectly claiming that the supplier should zero-rate its supplies to the charity, there will be a penalty equal to the difference between the tax which should have been chargeable on the supply and the amount actually charged.

9.5.4   Misdeclarations in VAT returns – s 63

Where there has been a serious misdeclaration in a VAT return, resulting in either an understatement of liability or an over-claim, there will be a penalty of 15% of the tax that would have been lost but for the discovery of the error. A serious misdeclaration occurs when the tax lost is more than the lower of £1m, or 30% of the aggregate of the true credit for input tax, and the true amount of output tax (the 'gross tax'). Voluntary disclosure by the taxpayer should not trigger a serious misdeclaration penalty, nor should a 'reasonable excuse'. Clearly this phrase will have to be defined by the courts, but it is likely only to include catastrophic circumstances over which the taxpayer has no control.

9.5.5   Persistent misdeclaration – s 64

If errors on subsequent returns occur in three or more periods within twelve accounting periods, to the extent of the lesser of £500,000 or 10% of the gross tax for the period, then a persistent misdeclaration penalty can be imposed. This will be 15% of the tax that would have been lost but for the discovery of the error. To discourage error, lower thresholds have been set so that the penalty bites when comparatively small errors occur.

9.5.6   Non-registration for VAT – s 67

A penalty will be incurred where the taxpayer fails to register for VAT when the statutory limits have been reached. Depending on the delay in applying for a registration, the penalty charged is either 5%, 10% or 15% of the tax that would have been due if registration had occurred at the right time. This rises to 20% if there has been a long period without proper registration.

9.5.7   Payment of interest on unpaid tax – s 74

This section gives details of interest that will be charged, in addition to penalties on outstanding amounts. Errors below £2,000, which are discovered by the charity and corrected before the next VAT return, will not attract interest.

This is a formidable array of weapons in Customs' hands and emphasises the point that accuracy and timeliness in the preparation of VAT returns is vital.

Chapter 10

CHARITIES AND VAT

'A veritable nightmare'

A former Director of Finance and Resources, Cancer Research Campaign

10.1   INTRODUCTION

As was seen in Chapter 9, VAT can be a veritable nightmare, unless one has an understanding of the basic principles of the tax, its pitfalls and penalties. Even then problems will remain. It is not necessary to have a profit motive to be within the scope of VAT. The fact that an activity being carried out by a charity is not trading for corporation and income tax purposes does not necessarily mean it is not a business supply for VAT purposes. Professional advice should always be sought on matters relating to VAT, particularly where large sums of the charity's money are involved.

Therefore, to repeat, charities are not exempt from paying VAT. All taxable supplies made in the course of business which is being carried out by an organisation registered for VAT are liable for VAT. This applies to charities as much as to any other business. Once registered, of course, a business (or charity) may be able to reclaim VAT paid on inputs, that is to say any items purchased which have VAT charged on them.

However, charities unlike most businesses, cannot recover all the VAT charged to them on goods and services. This is primarily because charities are involved in fundraising and similar activities which, as discussed at **10.6**, are outside the scope of VAT. Therefore, the VAT on the costs involved in carrying out these activities cannot be reclaimed.

The use of a trading subsidiary can simplify the process of dealing with VAT for a charity by having all the VAT-bearing activities concentrated in one area. If possible, the charity should then be left making only exempt supplies or those supplies which are outside the scope of VAT. Unfortunately, whilst this is fine in theory, it does not always work in practice.

That the VAT status of a trading activity is not affected by the type of organisation conducting the trade; for example, exemption for one-off fundraising events is available to any charity as well as to a wholly owned subsidiary of a charity, and the zero-rating applicable to donated goods is available for both the charity and its trading subsidiary.

Registration of both a charity and its trading subsidiary(ies) can be made individually or by means of a group registration. For separate registration, each organisation would need to show that its business income was over the annual threshold, although as we have seen earlier,[1] voluntary registration of the charity might be granted by HM Customs and Excise. If a charity and its trading subsidiary are separately registered, any charges between the two bodies will be subject to VAT if a taxable supply is made.

However, where a group VAT registration is in force, internal charges are outside the scope of VAT and only one VAT return will need to be completed for the group. In order for there to be a group VAT registration, the parent charity must itself be an incorporated body, ie a company. However, as all members of a VAT group are equally liable for the full net debt of the group, the charity may be granting a guarantee to its subsidiary concerning this debt. This could raise problems with the Charity Commission.

A VAT group registration may not increase the VAT recovery of the constituent parts and could inhibit the protection of the limited liability status of the trading company if that company becomes insolvent with unpaid VAT due to HM Customs and Excise. The views of the Charity Commissioners on the subject of group registration need to be considered very seriously. It is understood that they would wish to see an indemnity from the subsidiary to the charity, where practicable, in cases where the charity has discharged the liability of the subsidiary.

It is possible to register voluntarily for VAT purposes when annual turnover is below the threshold. Once registered, a charity is able to reclaim VAT paid on relevant inputs, that is to say any items purchased which have VAT charged on them. However, the charity will have to charge VAT on all its taxable supplies and will have to make VAT returns.

Any voluntary registration application cannot be backdated by more than three years; this is to bring the voluntary registration rules into line with the refund capping rules for businesses already registered. The three-year cap will not apply in the case of obligatory registrations.

10.2   COMMON TERMS/DEFINITIONS

VAT legislation is based on the concept of a supply of goods or services being made in the course of a business. Unfortunately, like 'trading' for corporation tax purposes, the word 'business' is not adequately defined in law. However, it does have a wider meaning than the word 'trading' and includes every trade, vocation or profession. A very useful source of information for charities when looking at VAT is provided by HM Customs and Excise VAT Notice 701/1/95, issued on 1 January 1995, and Update No 1 issued in February 1997, both of which are entitled '*Charities*', and give some very helpful definitions including:

---

1   In Chapter 9.

- *Outside the Scope* – activities not covered by VAT law, for example non-business ones or those carried on outside the European Union;
- *Exempt* – within scope of VAT but no VAT is charged when making these supplies – if only making exempt supplies cannot register and cannot recover VAT incurred on costs;
- *Zero Rate* – rate of VAT which is nil, ie no VAT charged on taxable supply but can register and recover VAT on costs.

Paragraphs 4 to 12 inclusive on pp 5–16 of this notice dealing with the definition of business and its application to charitable activities should be read thoroughly. It is essential that a clear understanding of this section is made because of the considerable effect on a charity's affairs if it is not.

Summarised in simple layman's terms there are effectively three kinds of relief from VAT: zero-rating, exemption and activities outside the scope. Although each has the effect of meaning that no VAT is charged on the supply, they are not synonymous. Where a charity makes a zero-rated supply, for example sale of donated goods, it is effectively charging VAT at zero per cent and can then recover any tax paid on input. However, where the supplies are exempt, for example interest on investments, no VAT is charged by the supplier and it is not possible to recover any tax paid on inputs. Similarly, no recovery may be made where the supply can be said to be outside the scope, for example legacy income. In these latter two cases there would effectively be a VAT cost to the charity, as it would be unable to recover any VAT incurred on inputs (expenditure) relating to the non-VATable outputs (income).

Therefore zero-rating for charities is very important because it helps to keep costs down and allows much more to be spent on the charitable objectives. However, not all goods and services that charities have to purchase are zero-rated, as we have seen, and this leaves most charities with the additional cost of what is called irrecoverable VAT.

Several businesses, and this includes many charities, have a mixture of outputs in all three categories. Effectively therefore, if they register in order to be in a position to recover VAT on costs incurred in making the VATable supplies, they will be 'partially exempt' because, of course, some of their supplies are exempt and some are not. This will be looked at in some detail at **10.9**.

An important distinction must be made between donations which are outside the scope of VAT (ie non-business) and sponsorship payments which may be. If the donor receives more than an insubstantial benefit, for example by way of publicity or facilities provided by the charity, the payment may be taxable because a supply is being made. Lotteries and raffles (where prizes are won by pure chance) are exempt from VAT, but most entry fees for competitions (where winning needs some skill) must include standard-rated VAT, unless the organiser is below the VAT registration threshold and is not registered for VAT.

Space precludes a completely exhaustive list of items that are zero-rated specifically for charities, or the full detailed conditions applying to that list.

Reference should be made to VAT Notice 701/1/95, pp 19–28. The list of zero-rated inputs (purchases) for charities in the UK is longer than that of any other country in the EU. When charities have particular problems they should obtain and read the appropriate leaflets, take professional advice and obtain clearance from their local VAT office where necessary.

10.3   SPONSORSHIP

As charity fundraisers come up with more and more new ideas for raising money, it can come as a nasty shock to find out that $\frac{7}{47}$ of the income might go to HM Customs and Excise instead. Sponsorship takes a variety of forms and can create as many difficulties. Sponsorship income may result from a genuine donation, a trading transaction or a mixture of the two. Put simply, if anything is supplied or deemed to have been supplied in return for financial support or sponsorship, a taxable supply has been made so far as HM Customs and Excise is concerned and VAT is payable. HM Customs and Excise do, like the Inland Revenue, accept that a payment, for which only an acknowledgement has been given, can be classed as a donation and therefore non-VATable as outside the scope.

If a contribution is made on the condition that a company's name or trading style is advertised or promoted, this constitutes advertising which is, of course, a VATable supply. Furthermore, if the company receives some other benefit in return, for example tickets to a gala concert, this too is a VATable supply. It will be standard-rated in both cases.

In essence, if the charity is providing anything in return for money received, VAT will become an issue. It is important therefore to think through agreements fully in advance. Care must also be taken in considering the VAT treatment of the provision of a charity's name and logo. In most circumstances, this would be viewed as a supply giving rise to standard-rated publicity services.

It may be that the sponsor concerned will agree to pay VAT on top of the payment he was going to make, particularly where he can recover the VAT within his own trading operation. Where a company takes an advertisement in a charity's annual report or programme that payment will be standard-rated because a supply has been made to the company, even if the company regards the payment as a donation.

Mixed deals, ie those where there is an element of both VATable and non-VATable supply taking place, should (if possible) be split, with the VATable supply put through a trading subsidiary and the non-VATable supply put through the charity. In other words, the donation goes to charity and the revenue from the commercial activity goes to the trading subsidiary. Obviously, this will not always be possible and where it is not, the charity is advised to put the complete transaction through the trading subsidiary to reduce the tax burden.

10.4   AFFINITY CARDS

One area particularly hard-hit by the addition of VAT was Affinity Credit Card schemes where charities had entered into agreements with banks, building societies and similar financial institutions. The issuing institution would make a 'donation' to the charity involved in respect of each card issued and for each occasion when the card was used. However this 'donation' had been decreed by HM Customs and Excise to be a payment in respect of promotional/advertising activities and as such a VATable supply. By a concession, negotiated by the CTRG, the income from such affinity credit cards is split into that part relating to a payment for services supplied by the charity, for example use of logo, mailing list, etc. and a donation for which the charity provides nothing in return, ie no VATable supply.

HM Customs and Excise had argued that the whole of the initial payment (often £5) and the percentage of turnover paid by the bank or similar institution to the charity, was taxable because it was paid in return for services provided by the charity. The CTRG was instrumental in bringing HM Customs and Excise and the Inland Revenue together and it was agreed that for contracts set up on the correct basis there could be, in effect, two separate legal arrangements. The first should be for 20% of the initial payment, which would then be taxable as a payment for services received; with a second agreement for the remainder, which would be outside the scope of VAT and treated as a donation, therefore neither VATable nor subject to corporation tax. Whilst this minimises the VAT and corporation tax, it does depend on carefully drafted contracts approved in advance by both HM Customs and Excise and Inland Revenue.

As seen when looking at the direct taxation aspects of such transactions, the arrangements for affinity cards should, wherever possible, be put through a trading subsidiary. Unless a contract specifies that a sum payable is exclusive of VAT, the law assumes that it is inclusive whenever VAT is due.[1]

10.5   DONATED GOODS

The sale of donated goods, for example through a charity shop, is a business activity and therefore a VATable supply is being made. However, such sales (discussed at **10.2**) are regarded as non-trading by the Inland Revenue and are currently zero-rated for VAT purposes, provided that they are made by a charity or by a taxable organisation which passes the profit to a charity. Prior to 1990, only certain classes of charities selling donated goods were allowed to zero-rate the sales.

---

1   See further VAT leaflet 701/41 entitled *Sponsorship*, which is a general leaflet not specifically aimed at charities.

Following the 1990 Budget, this provision was extended to apply to trading subsidiaries covenanting all the profit to a charity established primarily for the relief of distress or for the protection or benefit of animals. In the Budget of the following year, the zero-rating of donated goods was further extended to allow all charities and their trading subsidiaries to receive the zero-rating relief. Probably the greatest advantage of zero-rating the sale of donated goods is that, as a result, all the VAT incurred on the costs of disposing of the donated goods is fully recoverable.

However, where a charity shop sells bought-in goods, for example Christmas cards, it must remember that these may be standard-rated. Again, therefore, if there is to be a mixture of donated and bought-in goods sold through a charity shop, it would be advisable, particularly where the bought-in goods are a VATable item, to set up a trading subsidiary to carry out these activities.

In the 2000 Budget, the Chancellor announced that, with effect from 1 April 2000, the existing rules were to be relaxed to zero-rate the sale by charities of donated goods to disabled people and people receiving means-tested benefits before first offering them to the general public. Additionally, zero-rating was extended to include the sale of those goods that are of too poor a quality to be sold to the public and to the hire of donated goods. Finally, it will no longer be necessary for the trading subsidiary selling donated goods to have a profit-shedding covenant in place.

10.6   ONE-OFF FUNDRAISING EVENTS

Charities often organise special events for both fundraising and public relations purposes. There are special rules regarding the tax treatment of these events and the ubiquitous one-off fundraising event exemption has many complexities. Charities and wholly owned subsidiaries of charities, which pay their profits across to the charity, are required to treat as exempt all the income raised from a one-off fundraising event. The exemption applies to all admission charges, the sale of commemorative brochures, the sale of advertising space in those brochures, sale of goods (eg T-shirts) at the event and sponsorship income in connection with the event. The event must be separate from and not form any part of a series or regular run of like or similar events.

The 2000 Budget has brought many changes to this exemption and HM Customs and Excise have published a very useful notice on this topic.[1] This replaced paragraphs 27–37 of Notice 701/1/95 with effect from 1 April 2000.

When considering fundraising of this nature, there are a number of points to consider:

–   Which events qualify?

1   VAT Notice 701/59.

- How often can they be organised?
- What about the location and geographical proximity to other events?
- What about national events?
- What about joint events?
- Which events do not qualify?
- Must the exemption be used?

A fundraising event is one organised and promoted exclusively to raise money for the benefit of the charity or qualifying body. Social events which make a profit incidentally do not fall within the exemption. People attending or participating in the event must be aware of its primary fundraising purpose. An event is an incident with an outcome or a result; activities of a semi-regular or continuous nature, such as the frequent operation of a shop or bar, cannot therefore be an event.

The list below, which is not exhaustive, sets out the views of HM Customs and Excise on the different kinds of events which may be held for fundraising purposes:

- ball, dinner dance, disco or barn dance;
- performance; for example concerts, stage productions, and other events which have a paying audience;
- film showing;
- fete, fair or festival;
- horticultural show;
- exhibition – including art, history, science, etc;
- bazaar, jumble sale;
- sporting participation (including spectators);
- sporting performance;
- games of skill, contests, quizzes;
- endurance participation;
- fireworks displays;
- dinner, lunch, barbecue;
- auction;
- raffle, lottery.

Eligible events are restricted to no more than 15 events of a similar type per year at any one location. Where a concert is repeated on successive evenings each performance is a separate event and counts towards the maximum number of 15 events allowed within the exemption. These restrictions are to prevent distortion of competition with other suppliers of similar events which do not benefit from the tax exemption.

Additionally there is a special rule for small-scale fundraising events (eg coffee mornings) which do not count towards the 15-event limit, provided that total gross takings do not exceed £1,000 in any one week.

'Location' is defined as the geographical area within which the fundraising activity takes place. Similar kinds of events held in different locations would qualify for exemption provided all other conditions were met. For example, several balls held by a national charity in different cities on the same day would qualify for relief. Clearly, events which need to be held in special premises, such as sports grounds, swimming pools or theatres are easy to define. Each of these will be accepted as a location. However, an event held in multi-use premises, such as a village hall, will need to be held in different villages or town boroughs in order to qualify.

An event organised by two or more charities, or two or more qualifying bodies, qualifies for exemption only if all the charities (including their trading subsidiaries) and qualifying bodies have organised, whether individually or with others, less than 15 exempt events, of that type, in that location, in the year. A joint event organised by a charity and a qualifying body is exempt only if the charity (including its trading subsidiaries) and the qualifying body have organised, whether individually or with others, less than 15 events in the year. However, a joint event organised by a charity or qualifying body and anyone else cannot be an exempt fundraising event, as only events organised exclusively by charities, their trading subsidiaries and qualifying bodies qualify for exemption.

Events that do not qualify for exemption include:

– each event which counts towards 16 or more of the same kind held at the same location during the financial year;
– an event which takes over £1,000. This will not qualify as a small-scale event but will count towards the 15-event allowance;
– events which only form part of a social calendar for members;
– asking the public for donations through street collections, flag days, etc. These are not events for the purpose of this relief;
– selling goods. This does not constitute an 'event' unless it is an organised bazaar or similar. Therefore the sale of goods through retail outlets is not eligible for relief under these provisions, even where all the proceeds are received by a charity.

Every event in a programme of 16 or more events will be taxable at the standard rate. The exemption applies only to 15 or fewer events of the same kind at a location, because to exempt the first 15 events in a longer sequence, risks distortion of competition as far as HM Customs and Excise is concerned. VAT exemption is mandatory for any event that fulfils all the conditions. An event which does not meet one or more of the conditions will not qualify for exemption as a fundraising event.

Events arranged by a professional fundraiser may qualify for exemption if the charity, trading subsidiary or qualifying body is the principal making the supply. However, if the agent charges or retains any part of the gross receipts, this constitutes consideration for agency services and will be subject to VAT. This applies even if the amount is less than or equal to the cost of arranging the event. A VAT-registered agent can recover the VAT on his own administration costs. However, any VAT incurred by the charity or qualifying body in connection with the event will not be recoverable, as would be the case if the charity or qualifying body itself had made all the arrangements for the event.

The fact that a fundraising activity is exempt from VAT and any profit will not be taxed, does not mean that charities can undertake it directly. In many cases the charity's governing document may preclude the charity having the necessary power. Where the charity has the power, the trustees nevertheless need to consider carefully the risks to the charity's property. The charity's assets have been given for its charitable purposes and should not be exposed to any serious or substantial risk of loss from fundraising activities. Risks which might be acceptable commercially will not necessarily be acceptable for a charity.

The Charity Commission strongly advises trustees to take professional advice before doing anything to expand the charity's direct fundraising activities in any way falling outside this new statutory direct tax exemption. It will normally be appropriate for all larger-scale activities to be conducted by a trading subsidiary rather than the charity itself.

Large-scale events such as celebrity concerts, sporting events, etc can be a valuable way of raising funds. However, experience shows that they also carry a high degree of risk and charity trustees should not normally permit the charity to undertake such activities directly. Instead, they could be carried out by a trading subsidiary of the charity, thereby protecting the charity from the risk of loss. In order for charities to take full advantage of the new tax regime, a wholly owned trading subsidiary of the charity can be set up, which passes all its profits to the charity. This subsidiary will be subject to VAT in the same way as a charity.

The weakness of this particular exemption remains the fact that any VAT incurred on the cost of putting on the one-off fundraising event is not recoverable. However, as these events should be producing a profit or surplus the exemption from charging VAT normally outweighs this irrecoverable cost.

10.7   ADVERTISING

In addition to the general rules for zero-rating of printed matter, there are special rules for charities. Advertising which is either for fundraising purposes or making known the charity's aims and objects is zero-rated. This means that the supplier should not charge VAT to a charity when it uses printed material to:

–   seek donations;
–   publicise fundraising events; or
–   give general information about the charity.

Following the imposition of VAT on general newspaper advertising in 1984, charities successfully campaigned for the retention of a zero rate for certain advertisements. Over the years the scope of the relief has widened to include broadcasting of advertisements as well as printed media advertisements. Concessionary zero-rating of certain types of printed matter has been variously allowed from time to time.

As a result of the Review of Charity Taxation in 1997–1999, the scope of the relief has been widened further. The concessions have also been extended and incorporated into a formal ESC. Charities can advertise very broadly and this covers television, cinema, billboards, the sides of buses and other vehicles, newspapers and printed publications. In each case, the space must be owned by a third party; thus, space on someone else's Internet site will also be covered by the relief. If space is sold to a charity for advertising on other items, such as beer mats or the reverse of till rolls, this will also be covered by the zero rate. However, the sale of the items themselves cannot be relieved of VAT, unless they are relieved under other provisions.

Furthermore, certain methods of advertising are excluded from this relief where they are not the supply of someone else's advertising time or space, or in the form of marketing and promotion. Therefore, the following are specifically excluded:

–   the design and preparation of a charity's own website;
–   advertising in, on or through a charity's own website, whether or not the website is owned, rented or loaned to the charity. For the same reason adverts in a charity's own magazine, notices, calendar, diary or shop window, etc do not qualify for relief;
–   marketing and advertising addressed to selected individuals or groups. This includes telesales and direct mail by post or e-mail. In practice, this will mean that items delivered by post (direct mail packages) will not be covered, although there may be relief for individual elements of the package under the provisions for printed matter and concessions, eg appeal letters;
–   supplies connected with adverts that a charity produces itself.

The preparation of an advertisement will qualify for relief provided it is intended that the advertisement will be placed in purchased advertising time, material or space. This covers, for example, the design of a poster or the filming or recording of an advertisement to be broadcast.

The goods and services must be closely linked to the design or production of the advertisement to qualify. This includes, for example:

–   a finished article, such as a film or soundtrack, or an element to be incorporated, eg a photograph or picture or a script or a soundtrack;
–   alternative versions of an advertisement produced to see which works best. These will all qualify for relief even if it is the intention that only one version will be used;
–   the conversion from one format to another, more suitable, format.

Continuing its original intention to facilitate charitable fundraising activities, HM Customs and Excise allows the zero-rating of the following items which are directly used in fundraising campaigns:

– collecting boxes;
– some stationery;
– lapel stickers/badges.

The concession extends to all kinds of boxes and receptacles for money. All collecting 'boxes' may be zero-rated provided they comply with the following two conditions:

(1) they must bear the name of the charity either by indelible printing or embossing or having raised letters, and
(2) they must be tamper proof, ie capable of being sealed.

Examples of the types of boxes which might comply with the above conditions are:

– moulded plastic collecting boxes;
– pre-printed card collecting boxes;
– wood and glass receptacles; and
– hollow wood or plaster models, whether table-top or floor-standing or for wall mounting.

General purpose buckets are not covered by the concession; however, specially designed tamper-proof bucket lids which are used to seal buckets, making them suitable for charity donation, are included in the relief. Additionally, bucket-shaped boxes, which cannot be used for anything except collecting donations of money, will also come within the scope of the relief.

Elaborate boxes which have an additional purpose, such as gaming or quiz machines, or have some form of mechanical entertainment will not come within the concession. However, boxes where a simple balance mechanism moves the money from one level to another or the weight of a coin causes it to roll in a helter-skelter fashion into the box are included in the relief.

General stationery supplied to charities is not covered by the relief. However, the concession allows the following supplies of printed matter to be zero-rated when supplied to a charity:

– pre-printed letters appealing solely for money for the charity;
– envelopes used in conjunction with appeal letters and for forward donations, provided they are overprinted with an appeal request related to that contained in the letter;
– collecting envelopes which ask for donations of money, and similar envelopes used by religious organisations in their planned giving schemes.

This concession also means that lapel stickers, emblems and badges which are to be given free to donors as an acknowledgement of money donated, and have a nominal value, can be purchased free of VAT by charities. This relief is restricted to small items designed to be worn on clothing and includes paper stickers, ribbons, artificial flowers (if these are used as a symbol of the charity) and metal pins and badges. Large items for decorating buildings, monuments, vehicles, etc will not be eligible for relief even if these are just bigger versions of a lapel badge.

Those emblems given in return for an anticipated donation of £1 or less are considered to be of nominal value. In practice, this would mean that the cost to the charity would be considerably less than £1 per unit. Where a charity makes lapel badges itself then it cannot have relief for goods bought to make them nor can other tokens to be given away be zero-rated.

As a result of the 2000 Budget, HM Customs and Excise issued a new notice dealing with 'Charity Advertising and goods connected with collecting donations'. This replaced paragraph 16(A)–(E) of Notice 701/1/95.

10.8   MEMBERS' SUBSCRIPTIONS

Many charities, whether they are registered for VAT or not, may be missing out on the opportunity to reduce the amount of VAT that they pay. A charity which is registered for VAT will often treat all subscription income as standard-rated for VAT purposes. It is in fact possible to identify the separate elements of benefit to members and, where specific benefits (such as receipt of newsletters) would normally qualify for zero-rating, the subscription can be apportioned accordingly. The result of this is that the charity declares VAT on a percentage of subscription income, thereby reducing VAT payments accordingly.

Other charities may not have registered for VAT on the basis that no taxable income is received. It may be possible, however, to demonstrate to HM Customs and Excise that the charity does receive some zero-rated subscription income and, accordingly, is eligible for VAT registration. In certain circumstances, it is possible to register retrospectively (up to a period of three years) for VAT which, in turn, enables recovery of VAT on certain expenditure, which would not have been available if there was no registration in place. In order to obtain the maximum refund, it is important to provide calculations for the recovery of VAT in a manner acceptable to HM Customs and Excise.

As a result of an announcement by HM Customs and Excise, with effect from 1 December 1999 there is an exemption for certain subscriptions. Basically, apportionment of subscription income should be treated as follows:

(1) Standard-rated:
  –   Consultancy;
  –   Advice.
(2) Zero-rated:
  –   Newsletters;

- Handbooks.
(3) Exempt:
- Training;
- Education.

10.9 PARTIAL EXEMPTION

As was discussed in Chapter 9, this is a particularly thorny problem for anyone involved since its introduction following the Partial Exemption VAT Act 1983. The law in the UK is based on Articles 17 and 19 of the EC 6th VAT Directive. Effectively, partial exemption is the result of a business making (from the point of view of VAT) taxable and non-taxable supplies. Any VAT incurred on costs relating directly to exempt outputs is *not* recoverable; only input tax related directly to taxable outputs is recoverable. However, this is where the complications arrive as VAT on items such as administration costs which are not directly attributable either to the taxable or the exempt outputs may in part be recovered. Many charities fall into the category of businesses which are partially exempt.

Income for charities from sources such as donations or legacies is in the main, exempt (or outside the scope) for VAT purposes. Thus, a large number of charities which only receive income from these sources will be totally exempt from charging VAT and will therefore suffer the consequences of being unable to recover any VAT on the expenditure they incur. This situation is changing continually. Many charities are now engaging in quasi-trading activities where the supplies (outputs) they make do come within the scope of VAT, either being VATable at standard rate (currently 17.5%) or zero-rated. One example of the latter is charity shops which in the main are selling donated goods.

The sale of donated goods is regarded by the Charity Commission as not trading, but merely a conversion of a donation into cash. The Inland Revenue takes a somewhat similar view and does not attempt to tax the profit earned by charities from this source of income. However, for VAT purposes, the sale of donated goods is treated as a business taxable supply, although currently zero-rated. This enables the charities which operate such shops to recover all the VAT on costs directly incurred in the operation of those shops and also, by the apportionment method, to recover some of the VAT on general administration and similar costs.

Unfortunately, as we have seen, business is not defined for VAT purposes, nor have the decided cases produced any general principles. In most charities, some activity is likely to be non-business. The VAT incurred on general overheads and expenses which cannot be directly identified with either business or non-business expenses must be apportioned in order to determine the percentage of VAT recoverable. Various methods can be used and, as the amounts involved can be considerable, the challenge is to calculate a method which operates in the charity's best interest but which is still acceptable to HM Customs and Excise.

It is suggested that charities regularly review the items which can be classed as business and experiment on the apportionment of the residue based on the previous year's accounts. It would be helpful and sensible to talk through the results with a VAT adviser, if the charity has one, provided of course they understand and know the charity's business. In agreeing the relevant method with HM Customs and Excise, it may be possible to recover input tax for previous periods. This is particularly relevant where the charity has previously been operating to an agreed method. Having sorted out the business/non-business split, one could be forgiven for thinking that the remainder of the VAT return would be simple. Life never is. Undoubtedly, some of the charity's business supplies will be exempt. Subject to some fairly inadequate *de minimis* levels, a charity with exempt supplies will be struck by the dreaded 'partial exemption' clause.

10.9.1   De minimis

The restrictions on partial exemption only apply if a significant amount of input VAT relates to exempt activity. If this activity is below certain limits, it is possible to recover all the input VAT, ignoring the fact that the organisation (charity) has some exempt supplies. In these cases the organisation (charity) will be defined as fully taxable. Where it can be shown that in the normal accounting period the exempt input tax is £625 or less per month on average, all such input tax in that period will be treated as attributable to taxable supplies.

If a charity makes exempt supplies only, it has no right to register for VAT and consequently would not be able to recover any VAT on expenditure. If a charity makes taxable and exempt supplies, it can register for VAT. The current *de minimis* requirements are that all VAT can be recovered by a charity which makes both exempt and taxable supplies, provided the VAT on expenses attributable to exempt activities is less than £625 per month on average and 50% of total input tax incurred. This means that a charity which makes relatively few taxable supplies gets very little VAT back. If the *de minimis* limit is exceeded, all 'exempt' VAT is disallowed, not just the amount in excess of the limit. Most, if not all, charities have non-business income, grants, donations, etc. Any VAT on costs attributable to this income is irrecoverable regardless of the amounts involved.

In addition, charities are able to ignore exempt input VAT relating to investment income and incidental rental income. If these sources of income are the charity's only exempt supplies, the charity will not have to check whether it is within the *de minimis* limits. Partial exemption, therefore, is a subject that needs very careful thought. Supplies (ie costs) which are 'partly used or to be used in making taxable supplies shall be identified[1] and the tax on these items has to be apportioned. Under current VAT law, there are two separate methods for apportioning the 'remaining tax'. The 'new' standard method came into effect as long ago as 1 April 1992, and can be adopted without reference to HM Customs and Excise. This states that 'a charity may claim such proportion of its non-attributable input tax as bears the same ratio to the total of such input tax as the value of its taxable supplies bears to the value of all its supplies'.

10.9.2   Apportionment

The amount of input tax which a taxable charity is entitled to deduct provisionally is the amount attributable to taxable supplies in accordance with the following rules:

(1) identify goods imported or acquired by, and goods or services supplied to, the taxable charity in the period;
(2) input tax on such of those goods and services as are used, or are to be used, by the charity exclusively in making taxable supplies is attributed to taxable supplies;
(3) no part of the input tax on such of those goods or services as are used, or could be used, by the charity in making exempt supplies, or in carrying on any activity other than the making of taxable supplies must be attributed to taxable supplies;
(4) a proportion of the remaining input tax on such of those goods and services as are used, or to be used, by the charity in making taxable and exempt supplies is to be attributable to taxable supplies calculated as follows:

$$\text{Remaining input tax} \times \frac{\text{value of taxable supplies}}{\text{value of all supplies}}$$

The ratio of the taxable supplies to the value of all supplies is to be expressed as a percentage and, if not a whole number, is to be rounded up to the next whole number.

There are a number of other methods, described as 'special methods', which HM Customs and Excise will accept as fair under their powers to approve calculation methods in advance. The previous standard method, under which non-attributable input tax was apportioned according to the use of the goods and services on which it was incurred, became a special method which will require the approval of HM Customs and Excise before it can be used, as a result in the change of the regulations in March 1992. However, if a charity had been using this method previously, and wished to continue to use it in the future, it would not have needed to take any action as the use would be

---

1   VAT Notice 706.

regarded as formally approved when the charity next received a visit by an officer from HM Customs and Excise.

Similarly, the 'new' standard method had formally been a special method; any charity which had been using it previously and wished to continue in the future also needed no formal approval. Obviously, any charity which had been using any other approved special method and wished to continue to use it could do so, subject only to a review by HM Customs and Excise.

The VAT laws and regulations do not explain concisely the way in which supplies are to be apportioned between taxable and exempt, although this is, of course, fundamental to any calculations. As a result, the split between taxable and exempt need not be based on financial values, and one can therefore, as in management accounting, resort to allocation on the basis of staff numbers, transaction numbers, floor areas, etc. In the case of special methods, whilst the ratio is still expressed as a percentage, it is done so *without* rounding up, as is the case for the standard method. A special method may also be based on separate calculations for different sectors of the business, or in the case of group registration, different businesses or groups of businesses within the VAT group. However, note that with any special method, HM Customs and Excise will attempt to make certain that they are not at a disadvantage.

Related to partial exemption is the Capital Goods Scheme (CGS), under which the affected charity will be required to adjust annually the input tax claimed in respect of high-value computer equipment or land and buildings, to the extent that the use of such assets is for exempt purposes. Currently, the limit in relation to computer equipment is over £50,000, and for land and buildings, over £250,000; which may be repayable if the extent to which the assets are used, or the partial exemption position, changes over a period of five years for computers or ten years for land and buildings. Another pitfall for charities which are partially exempt relates to the self-supply of stationery and printed matter. A partially exempt organisation which produces printed matter for use in its own business is liable to account for output tax on the value of that stationery.

At present, partially exempt organisations have to reach agreement with HM Customs and Excise on a basis for apportioning the input tax they have paid out between exempt and non-exempt supplies. Disagreements arise over the treatment of overheads, which relate to both exempt and non-exempt sides of the business. The deductions of input tax for each prescribed accounting period are provisional, whichever method is adopted. This is because the amount deductible in some such periods may be unfairly affected, for example seasonal variations through Christmas card sales. It is therefore normally necessary to recalculate the amount of input tax reclaimable over a somewhat longer period. If a special method is used, the letter of approval from HM Customs and Excise will state whether an annual adjustment is required.

All in all, this is a very complex subject and one which needs to be carefully monitored to avoid statutory penalties. As this is one of the most dangerous and difficult areas of VAT, it is vital to discuss any suggestions with professional VAT advisers. A thorough read of HM Customs and Excise VAT Notice 706 *Partial Exemption* is recommended for all charity officials.

10.10   PROPERTY

The VAT position on property has changed considerably in the last 16 years or so, with significant effect on charities. As a result of FA 1984, alterations became standard-rated (except for some special work on protected buildings) where previously they had been zero-rated. Then in 1989, to comply with the decision reached in the European Court of Justice on 21 June 1988, the UK Government was forced to extend the scope of VAT at the standard rate and to include the supply of non-residential buildings and associated construction services.

The effect of these changes to the VAT regulations is that zero-rating is now confined to sales of the freehold or the grant of a long lease by the person or persons constructing dwellings, some other residential buildings (eg old people's homes) and certain properties for non-business charitable use, and to construction services relating to these buildings.

HM Customs and Excise VAT Notice 742A on property development points out that the first supply of a new building will be zero-rated if:

–   the building qualifies;
–   the relevant certificate from the purchaser or lessee has been supplied;
–   the supplier grants a major interest in all or part of the building or its site; and
–   the building is new rather than the conversion, reconstruction, alteration, enlargement or extension of an existing building.

All these conditions have to be met and, if only part of the building is eligible for zero-rating, it would be necessary to apportion the consideration received when it is disposed of.[1]

Effectively three types of building qualify for zero-rating:

(1)   a domestic dwelling;
(2)   a building used for a relevant residential purpose; and
(3)   a building used for a relevant charitable purpose.

VAT Notice 742A *Land and Property* – gives examples of a wide range of buildings which qualify under 'relevant residential purpose'. They include children's homes; homes for the old and disabled; hospices; living accommo-dation for students or school children; living accommodation for members of

---

1   See VAT Notice 701/1/95 *Charities*, p 22.

the armed forces, etc. However, hospitals, prisons, hotels, inns, etc are not included.

The definition given in the guidance notice of a 'relevant charitable purpose' effectively means that the building must be used by the charity otherwise than in the course of business, or as a village hall or community hall providing social or recreational facilities. Of course, many buildings used by charities may well also qualify under the relevant residential purpose qualification. Any type of building can qualify, but the restriction on business use is important, as HM Customs and Excise's interpretation of business is very wide.

Therefore, the VAT legislation allows supplies, made in the course of construction of a building intended for use solely for a relevant charitable purpose, to be zero-rated. Supply must be made to the organisation (ie charity) which intends to use the building. Services of architects, surveyors, or any other persons acting as a consultant or in a supervisory capacity do not qualify for zero-rating;[1] and these services are therefore standard-rated. However, as a planning idea, it is possible for the contractor to agree a design and building contract, which would allow such services, supplied under the contract, to be zero-rated as the service is all-inclusive. In addition, supplies of materials, builders' hardware, sanitary ware and other articles of a kind ordinarily installed by builders as fixtures may also be zero-rated, provided they are supplied by the person supplying the construction services.

Provided all the conditions set out above have been met, the charity must give to its contractors a certificate stating that the supply, or part of it, may be zero-rated. This certificate must be given to the contractor prior to the commencement of construction services. Penalties can be enforced against the wrongful issue of such certificates. The amount of the penalty is 100% of the tax chargeable had the service not been zero-rated. This is a particularly severe penalty and extreme caution should be taken before a charity issues such a certificate. Zero-rating is not applicable in respect of construction services relating to:

– the conversion, reconstruction, alteration or enlargement of an existing building; or
– an extension or annexation to an existing building which provides for internal access to the existing building or of which the separate use, letting or disposal is prevented by the terms of a covenant, statutory planning or similar permission.

As a concession, HM Customs and Excise allow insignificant non-charitable use of a building to be disregarded in assessing whether zero-rating should apply. For the purposes of this concession, 'insignificant' is deemed to be no more than 10% of the time that the building is available for use. Historically, the application of this particular concession has been inconsistent and different

1   See further VAT Notice 701/1/95 *Charities*, p 22, para 20.

HM Customs and Excise offices have used different methods of calculating the level of business use.

As the intention of the concession was to soften the impact of the full test by disregarding insignificant non-qualifying use, it has now been formalised. With effect from 1 June 2000, the measurement of business use can be calculated in one of the four following ways:

(1) time based – entire building only;
(2) time based – parts of a building only;
(3) floor space – entire building only;
(4) head count – entire building only.

Although the first method does not require prior written approval from HM Customs and Excise, the last three do. In other words, whether a building qualifies for zero-rating will depend very much on the specific details of each case. However, a charity may, following approval where applicable, use any one of the four methods. A charity will need to choose the method that most favours its own circumstances. HM Customs and Excise offices have been advised not to refuse to approve an application simply because an alternative method is available.

In general, alterations to residential or charitable buildings are standard-rated. However, there are two main exceptions to this:

(1) approved alterations to protected buildings are zero-rated;
(2) certain alterations supplied to handicapped persons or to a charity providing facilities for the handicapped. These will include:

  – provision of toilet and bathroom facilities;
  – installation of lifts;
  – construction of ramps or widening of doors or passages to facilitate entry or movement.

The 2000 Budget extended the existing VAT relief on bathrooms to cover adaptions or extensions in day care centres where 20% or more of the users are disabled. The provision, adaption or extension of bathrooms for disabled people in sheltered flats and houses where the landlord is a charity, is also covered.

Simplified VAT rules on property, land and construction, introduced in the 1994 Budget to help the construction industry, have enabled charities to reduce costs. The main measures, introduced with effect from 1 March 1995, were zero-rating of the first grant of a major interest by the developer of a building converted from non-residential property into dwellings; clarification of the distinction between new and existing buildings; repeal of the developers' self-supply charge on business property and simplification of the rules on business rents.

There are claw-back provisions if the conditions for zero-rating are breached up to ten years after the completion of construction of a new building.[1] Effectively, if the building is sold or a lease is granted within the ten-year period, this would be treated as a standard-rated supply and VAT must be charged on any consideration received, unless the vendor obtains a certificate from the purchaser stating that the qualifying use will continue. However, if there is a change of use in the building, there is a deemed self-supply for VAT purposes. The value of the self-supply is such that the amount of output VAT which must be accounted for is equal to the VAT which would have been due but for the original zero-rating.

Charities must take care to ensure that they are aware of the implications of a change of use to some or all of a building which they occupy. In many cases, what was originally regarded as a minor activity and therefore within the *de minimis* rules, may become significant and would then be regarded by HM Customs and Excise as a business activity. For example, a charity may set up a small trading operation selling Christmas cards which contribute a very small proportion of the charity's total income. However, after five or ten years this may no longer be the case; the income would now be coming from trading and in this case the business activity could exceed the 10% rule.

It is quite clear that the onus is on the charity to notify HM Customs and Excise of any change in use but, in the past, Customs have pointed out that they will make inspections during the ten-year period for both VAT-registered and unregistered charities. Failure to notify changes could result in severe penalties for misdeclaration and, where the charity was not registered, further charges for late registration if the VAT involved triggers the registration threshold.

A charity that uses its own resources to construct a qualifying building other than in the course of business will be able to make a claim for repayment of VAT incurred on goods or materials under s 35 of VATA 1994. This provision allows charities to construct their own buildings, for example, with the use of volunteers, at no VAT disadvantage. However, the relief applies only where the building would have been zero-rated; therefore it must be a new building, not an alteration or extension to an existing one, and must be used as a dwelling or for a qualifying purpose.

One very significant advantage of self-supply is that the regulations contain no claw-back provision in the event of disposal or change in use during the following ten years, in contrast to the provisions of VATA 1994 in respect of purchased new buildings.[2]

Where a charity is substantially reconstructing a protected building for use as a dwelling or for another qualifying purpose, it will be able to zero-rate the sale of

---

1   See further VAT Notice 708 *Buildings and Construction.*
2   See further VAT Notice 719 *VAT refunds to 'do it yourself' builders.*

the freehold or the grant of a long lease.[1] To qualify as an approved alteration to a protected building the works must be:

- approved, which effectively means that they require approval under all the various Planning Acts, unless of course the building is an ecclesiastical building, in which case any alteration qualifies; and
- an alteration, as opposed to repairs and maintenance. As is usual in these matters the definition of an alteration is not given and the dividing line between an alteration and a repair is very thin.

One of the peculiarities in VAT law is the charging of VAT on rents. Many charities may find themselves in rented property either as landlord or tenant. Normally the grant of a lease and the premiums and rents payable are exempt supplies for VAT purposes. However, since 1 August 1989 certain supplies, which would otherwise have been exempt, can now be treated as standard-rated. Effectively owners and landlords can now elect to waive the requirement to exempt from VAT certain supplies of buildings and land. Thus, the owner or landlord decides whether or not to charge VAT on the rent.

This facility is commonly referred to as 'the option (or "election") to tax'. However, note that once an election has been made it cannot be revoked for a period of twenty years. It is also worth pointing out that an election will apply to a whole building and cannot be split. Thus, where the building has one or more tenants, either all or none of them will be charged VAT. It is felt that the main purpose in electing to waive exemption on a supply is to enable the supplier to recover input tax on any related expenditure. The general rule is that input tax incurred before the option takes effect cannot be reclaimed in full; however, this does not apply where the supplier has not made any exempt supplies in relation to the land or buildings concerned before the election has taken effect.

These changes may have had a significant impact on charities. The option to tax is that of the landlord; the tenant has no role in the decision. Therefore, charities which are wholly or partly exempt will suffer an irrecoverable VAT cost in renting an opted property. However, the option cannot be exercised in respect of any building intended solely for qualifying residential or charitable use and, therefore, a charity can avoid VAT on the rent on such buildings if they are used for non-business purposes. Where the charity takes over an existing building that is subject to the option to tax, the option will not apply if the charity uses the building for non-business purposes and issues a certificate to confirm said use.

In the position of landlord, a charity has, of course, the option to tax any properties which it is letting. This could have significant advantages:

- it allows full recovery of input VAT on costs directly attributable to the property; and

---

1   Attention should be paid to VAT Notice 708 *Buildings and Construction.*

–   it increases the partial exemption recovery rate, thus increasingly residual VAT recovery.

However, the decision on whether or not to tax will need to take account of whether the tenants themselves are fully taxable, as the commercial disadvantage of having to tax the rents may outweigh the benefits of recovering input tax. When considering the option to tax, the impact on the total level of taxable supplies then being made by the charity must be taken into account also, as this may possibly trigger a requirement to register.

Furthermore, anti-avoidance legislation can prevent an option to tax having effect where:

–   the building is or will become a capital item within the Capital Goods Scheme for either the person selling, granting a lease of or a licence to occupy it, or for any person to whom the building is sold or transferred before it has become a capital item;
–   the grant is made before the building ceases to be within the Capital Goods Scheme; and
–   at the time of the grant the person making the grant, or any person funding that person's cost of acquiring, constructing or refurbishing the building, intends or expects that the property will be occupied, or if already occupied will continue to be occupied, by any of the following other than wholly or mainly for taxable business purposes:
    –   the person making the grant;
    –   the person funding the person making the grant;
    –   a person connected with either of them.

The above provision also covers any grant made between 19 March 1997 and 10 March 1999, if at the time of the grant there was no capital item in existence but the person who made the grant intended or expected it would become one. However, the new provision affects only supplies arising from the grant made on or after 10 March 1999.[1]

10.11   GROUPS

As previously noted, registration of both a charity and its trading subsidiary(ies) can be made individually or by means of a group registration.

HM Customs and Excise, having reviewed the VAT group facility to see if it is possible to achieve, as they put it, 'a better balance between revenue costs to the Exchequer and compliance costs for businesses', decided to introduce 'a more flexible and efficient VAT system for business'.[2] Changes were announced during the 1999 Budget that have been effected by amendment to VATA 1994. The main details are as follows:

---

1   For more details see para 8.4 of HMCE Notice 742A – *Land and property*.
2   Press release and VAT Notice 700/2 – *Group Treatment*.

– removing the requirement for organisations to give 90 days' notice when they apply to form, join, leave or disband a VAT group;
– giving HM Customs and Excise the power to remove groups, companies that are no longer eligible to be grouped or whose membership of a group proposes a threat to the Revenue;
– changing the eligibility criteria relating to territorial scope (ie whether a company has a sufficient presence within the UK to be eligible for grouping); and
– extending operations' rights of appeal in respect of grouping.

Further details were included in VAT Notice 700/2.

10.12   CONCLUSIONS

Charities benefit from a wide range of tax and VAT exemptions and their proper use can maximise income and reduce costs. A charity can often use the exemptions given to donors to persuade the donor to give more. Charity administrators and trustees should make sure they are correctly informed and updated in respect of tax and charity law, and keep detailed records of all income and expenditure.

ADDENDUM TO CHAPTER 10

SUMMARY OF SPECIAL VAT RELIEFS FOR CHARITIES

A   Supplies by charities

(1)   Outside the scope/non-business
The following are regarded as non-business activities and are therefore outside the scope of VAT:

–   voluntary services;
–   grants;
–   welfare services made at below cost – there is a requirement that these should be at least 15% below cost and effectively be funded by the charity's own resources;
–   voluntary contributions including donations and legacies;
–   membership subscriptions to a charity that provides no personal benefit.

(2)   Exempt
–   interest;
–   welfare supplies (otherwise than for profit);
–   sales from hospital trolleys (but not to staff or visitors);
–   acknowledgement 'advertisements' (regarded as donations but see below);
–   nursing home supplies;
–   donation element of affinity card payments (but see standard-rated below);
–   one-off fundraising events.

(3)   Zero-rated
–   sale of donated goods (via charity shops or otherwise);
–   exports.

(4)   Standard-rated
–   catering;
–   meals on wheels;
–   advertisements;
–   affinity cards;
–   sponsorship (where consideration given in return).

The lists given above are examples only; as can be clearly seen, some supplies may fall into more than one category. This is particularly true where the charity provides something in return, ie it actually makes a supply of a service or goods. Advertisements, affinity cards and sponsorship, in particular, fall into a grey area.

B   Supplies to charities

The following supplies to charities are zero-rated (see also C below):

–   advertisements, for making known the charity's objectives or for the purpose of raising funds. This includes advertising in printed matter, cinema, radio and television:[1]
–   building works – relevant charitable purpose;
–   drugs and chemicals – used directly in human medical research;
–   recording equipment, talking books and newspapers for the blind.

C   Legislation

Schedule 8 to VATA 1994, which came into force on 1 September 1994, has many sections dealing with charities, in particular:

> Group 4 – eg zero rating of purchase or hire of talking books.
> Group 5 – eg zero rating of charitable purpose new buildings.
> Group 6 – extends Group 5 to cover reconstructions.
> Group 7 – relates to fuel and power.
> Group 8 – eg zero rating relating to lifeboats.
> Group 12 – large and complex section dealing with concessions to handicapped persons.
> Group 15 – eg advertising concessions.

It is therefore essential for all those involved with the finances of charities to read thoroughly VATA 1994 and the relevant schedules.

---

1   But see **10.7**.

Chapter 11

FUTURE DEVELOPMENTS

'Nothing can be said to be certain, except death and taxes.'

Benjamin Franklin, 1789

11.1   INTRODUCTION

Although the actual process of changing taxation is complex, we do need to examine the reliefs available to charities, as well as the mechanisms that support them, in the light of whether they are really the most effective way to deal with particular problems. Throughout this book, we have looked at the reliefs available to charities but, rather than taking tax relief for granted, we should begin by questioning whether there should be tax relief for charities at all. From time to time in the general media there are lengthy debates about this particular question, the most recent being the charity tax review which culminated in the 2000 Budget and the lengthy document *'Getting Britain Giving'*.

11.2   WHY SHOULD CHARITIES RECEIVE SPECIAL TREATMENT FROM THE TAX SYSTEM?

There are a number of arguments against any special treatment, the first of which is aimed at donor reliefs. This maintains that giving to charity is a private voluntary act and equates it with the purchase of goods. The argument is therefore propounded that it is wrong for the State to intervene in this process of free choice by favouring one against the other, since this distorts the market which, economists argue, works most efficiently when it is free of interference.

The second part of the argument, or indeed a separate argument which is aimed at donor reliefs and charity organisation reliefs maintains that reliefs of any kind create difficulties for the tax system, making it more complicated than it already is and creating opportunities for avoidance. Indeed, a number of years ago, leading Labour politicians were of the view that charities were simply tax avoidance vehicles.

The third and final argument raised against special tax reliefs for charities is that providing shelter for charities from the full rigour of the tax code is an expenditure of public money. This is because it has the effect of reducing the amount of tax gathered and that this shortfall then has to be provided by the general taxpayer. It continues that public funds should not be spent without explicit choice, strict control and scrutiny. Effectively, the argument is that expenditure via the granting of reliefs means that public control of the use of funds is lost.

Those supporting these arguments consider that the provision of tax reliefs to charities has led to a large increase in the number of organisations of which many provide dubious benefit and at worst could be considered to be a social nuisance. Why, for example, they argue, should a taxpayer who may be totally irreligious subsidise the advancement of religion? They argue that these increases in the number of charities and charitable activity would not have happened if the prize of tax relief had not been available.

Obviously, for all the arguments against tax relief for charities, there are counter-arguments in favour of continuing and even extending tax relief for charities and donations to charities. The views are probably really all variations on what may be said to be the social benefit argument. This sits against the harsh commercial view expressed earlier but, unlike other types of private expenditure, donations to charities produce external benefits for society as a whole in the form of the activities of charitable organisations which would not otherwise take place.

Effectively, individuals are encouraged to care for their fellow individuals and tax relief encourages socially beneficial behaviour. To encourage this, it is therefore perfectly right and proper that the tax system lends a little assistance both in encouraging donors and in assisting the charities themselves. It is in fact true to say that most of the charities would exist whether or not there was tax relief but would possibly be rather worse off. Many of them, for example medical research charities, are providing benefits to society that should otherwise be provided by the State. Many other charities, for example the Royal National Lifeboat Institution, provide a service which the Government has a legal liability to ensure it is in place. The Government has often declined to take a positive role in certain areas so it is right that it provides some form of assistance for others to provide that role.

This will enable charities to grow and flourish and tax exemption is therefore more likely to produce constructive and creative responses to the problems of a rapidly changing society than a rigid application system for explicit Government support. Another vital point made by supporters of tax relief to charities is that it is not expensive; indeed, it may generate benefits well in excess of the costs. In this way tax rates for the general taxpayer are kept low because tasks that would have been taken on by the public sector are carried out by the private sector, ie the charities.

Against the criticism that public funds are not being properly controlled, it could be said that a direct, voted subsidy to specific charities could lead to charges of favouritism and even corruption. This issue has been raised in relation to the distribution of funds by the National Lottery. The present system of tax reliefs does not discriminate between different charities and the level of tax relief depends on a charity's own efforts; for example, the more Gift Aid donations it receives, the higher the tax relief it obtains.

It seems unlikely that the principle of tax relief for charities will be abolished. Indeed, it is being extended. In any event, no political party is suggesting that it should be reduced. However, the effect of membership of the EU has to be taken into account and the varying types of relief currently available to charities could change.

11.3   EUROPEAN INFLUENCES – VAT

11.3.1   Background

The economic and total integration of the Member States of the EU is having and will continue to have far-reaching implications for the charitable sector. It is probable that the most important development so far has been the move towards what was originally described as harmonisation of the VAT rates. These moves could have very seriously jeopardised the hard-won concessions on VAT which UK charities then did and still do enjoy. The abolition of zero rates would have had disastrous effects, trebling the irrecoverable VAT bills of many charities. The aim of the European VAT harmonisation scheme is the eventual introduction of the original system for the collection of VAT. Effectively, this would mean that each product or service would bear VAT according to the rate levelled in its country of origin. The original intention that this would come into effect from 1 January 1993 was subsequently postponed to 1 January 1997, and has now been postponed again but with the permanent VAT regime to be introduced by 2002. We are, therefore, in what is called the 'transitional period'. During this time VAT will continue to be levied according to the destination principle and effectively all UK zero rates, including those enjoyed by charities, will be safeguarded, at least as far as the EU is concerned.

The CTRG was established in 1981 by eight charities which were very concerned about the impact of irrecoverable VAT on the services they provided. Now representing over 300 leading charities, the Group's objective is the improvement in the fiscal treatment of registered charities and similar bodies through representations to Government, HM Customs and Excise and the Inland Revenue. Although CTRG's primary aim is to see VAT relief extended to all goods and services supplied to charities, it also covers direct tax issues and, where appropriate, matters of charity law.

For many years CTRG has worked closely with a number of European networks, most notably those in fields dealing with the blind, cancer research, heart disease, lifeboat and development organisations. Recognising, as it did, that any final solution to the VAT problems of charities would have to come from Europe, CTRG towards the end of 1992 organised an important meeting in Brussels to discuss how to resolve this problem. Out of this meeting, which was attended by 60 representatives of charities from ten Member States, a new group was set up (the European Charities Committee on VAT (ECCVAT)), to discuss VAT-related issues, carry out research and organise lobbying campaigns as and when necessary.

As far as VAT is concerned, harmonisation is the great threat on the horizon. The most probable impact of this is a trebling of irrecoverable VAT for charities. Again, thanks to the interim Directive, it was agreed that the final harmonisation be put off until at least 2002. The preservation of those zero rates in force on 1 January 1991 should only apply, according to some EU officials, provided they meet both the following criteria laid down in the Directive:

(1) That they are for clearly defined social reasons.
(2) That they are for the benefit of the final consumer.

CTRG believes quite keenly that, should this position be pursued, *all* charities could lose some or many of the zero rates that they currently enjoy. It should also be pointed out that concessions granted in 1991 and 1992 budgets which further extended VAT zero rates most certainly infringe this particular Directive. The range of goods and services to which the UK Government has over the years extended zero-rating for charities specifically is very extensive. It includes such things as:

- advertising for fundraising purposes;
- drugs and chemicals used directly in human or animal medical research;
- talking books and newspapers for the blind;
- certain building works for relevant charitable purposes;
- some sea rescue equipment;
- various donated medical and scientific equipment;
- certain equipment for handicapped persons;
- sale of donated goods.

It is impossible here to produce an exhaustive list or to provide the full detailed conditions applying to that list. Suffice it to say that the list of zero-rated inputs (purchases) for charities in the UK is longer than that of any other country in the EU. Indeed, since only four other EU countries have zero rates, the UK list is certainly as long as all the others put together. Thus, it is quite clear what effect VAT harmonisation would have on the UK charity scene. The impact would be enormous; for example, in the case of the Cancer Research Campaign, the removal of zero-rating on the sale of donated goods could cost them £2m per annum. Harmonisation, ie the withdrawal of *all* zero rates and their replacement with a standard rate of 17.5%, would cost the Cancer Research Campaign at least an additional £3m to £4m per year.

One must also mention that little known item, at least as far as the UK is concerned, of 'reduced rate bands' on which discussions continue behind closed doors within the EU. There must be a solution here for charities if zero rates are to disappear but only if some very difficult negotiations succeed. The particular concerns in these negotiations relate to the definition of charity; the organisations to be covered by that definition; the range of goods and services to be included; the rate to be applied; and, most importantly, whether or not in the particular case of charitable and welfare items both inputs (purchases) and outputs (sales) are covered.

Unfortunately, at the early stages, the drafting seemed to indicate that whilst outputs were in, inputs might well be out. UK charities could find that much of the range of goods which they are at present able to purchase at the zero rate of VAT, moves from a zero rate to a standard rate, bypassing the reduced rate. Following extensive lobbying by CTRG, ECCVAT and the European networks with which they work, it was agreed that charity and welfare services should be in the list of items eligible for inclusion in the reduced rate category. CTRG is continuing to work very hard to ensure that the definition of these services is sufficiently comprehensive to cover the current VAT reliefs on both inputs and outputs of charities.

Many Ministers and senior EU officials have shown little willingness to support amendments to the 6th Directive which would have greatly eased the burden on charities. In fact they have indicated that it is unlikely that VAT relief for charities can be granted through the VAT system, which is why the idea of a refund mechanism was proposed by ECCVAT and CTRG as the simplest and most effective way of helping charities with their VAT bills. The proposal was to compensate charities for all or part of their VAT burden incurred on inputs as well as outputs. This compensation would not probably form part of the VAT system but would be regarded as part of public expenditure. Obviously, before one can get to this stage, there would need to be an agreement at EU level to avoid a situation where those Member States which are not prepared to introduce the reform argue against implementation in other Member States on the grounds that it would distort competition. There is much work to be done in this area.

The future on VAT for charities looks bleak indeed and much remains to be done to persuade the EU, with the help of UK MEPs and Government, to obtain the best deal possible for charities. A lot of work needs to be carried out to ensure that if zero rating is lost, those purchases to which it currently applies are either included in the reduced rate bands, or a refund mechanism, as above, is introduced throughout Europe. CTRG and ECCVAT will be continuing this battle.

11.3.2 VAT Directives

In 1993, a headline screamed 'EC VAT charge could cost charities £25m'. This seems as good a point as any to start with when considering the implications of European Directives on the sale of donated goods by charities. That particular headline referred to selling donated goods. The UK is still the only member of the EC that has applied a zero-rate of VAT on the sale (output) of donated goods by charities.

As is well known, the UK is a major proponent of zero-rated VAT, applying it not only to donated goods but also to items such as children's clothing, books, transport and many food items. However, few of the other 14 members of the EU have any form of zero-rating and the use in those countries where it does exist is not particularly wide ranging. The UK, it appears, stands alone in its opposition to this particular Directive. It is difficult, therefore, to get support from the other Member States for the proposed retention of zero-rating for donated goods sold through charity shops.

The original proposal was that VAT should be levied on the selling price of second-hand goods. A number of other proposals have subsequently been debated and it is to be hoped that the UK margin scheme will be the one finally adopted. It would be totally unrealistic to imagine that the UK can hang on to zero rates indefinitely, but this proposal, which seeks to charge the tax on the margin between the purchase and the selling price of second-hand goods, might be an improvement on the original proposal.

However, although this is effectively a tax on the value added, which therefore ties in with the main principle of VAT, it does mean that for charities selling donated goods this would equate to a VAT charge on the selling price since the purchase price of donated goods is obviously zero! There is an overall acknowledgement that even if the zero-rate is protected during the transitional period, the position of charities will still be jeopardised.

CTRG continued to argue for a scheme to amend the 7th Directive which would have the effect of decreasing the selling price so that it was equal to the purchase price for donated goods. In other words, the margin on which the standard rate of VAT would then be applied would be zero. The logical argument supporting this proposal is that it would avoid double taxation of the goods and show that there is no margin to tax because there has effectively been no value added.

Although UK charities are safeguarded by the transitional protection until it ends, charity shops will be saddled thereafter with a permanent Directive which requires them to suffer VAT on donated goods. Obviously, a charity can either attempt to recoup the VAT imposed by putting up its prices which could result in lost sales, or it could leave prices where they are and thus suffer a reduced profit. OXFAM has claimed that this imposition would reduce its total net income by about 10% (a figure of £6m per annum), which it stated was equivalent then to its entire annual grant programme to 21 African countries. This would, therefore, amount to a considerable imposition, but in fairness not one affecting all charities because not all have shops selling donated goods.

It appears that, although this Directive may go ahead with VAT being charged on the selling price, it is likely to be charged at a reduced rate, possibly of 5.5%. However, will the UK accept further reduced rates?

11.4   CONCLUSIONS

The complexities in VAT arise principally from the mixture of business and non-business activities which most charities undertake. As was discussed at Chapter 4, there may be advantages to putting all the business activity through a trading subsidiary. This subsidiary would most probably be wholly owned by the charity, but it is unlikely that it would have been set up specifically and simply for VAT reasons. When looking at this question one needs to have regard to the other legal implications, in particular those relating to corporation tax and the Charity Commission.

Fortunately, the EU has not so far seriously involved itself in direct taxation, although there have been discussions. The UK is probably the most generous member in its protection of charities from direct tax particularly following the 2000 Budget. Although other Member States are not as favourably disposed to charities as the UK Government in relation to direct tax, the position is far better than it is for VAT. Gifts to charities are exempt from IHT only in Denmark, France, Germany, Ireland, Italy, Luxembourg, Portugal and Spain. Only in Belgium and Holland is tax levied on gifts to charities. Some countries are more generous to the individual or company donor than in the UK. Therefore, if there is ever to be direct tax approximation within the European Union, charities should not suffer quite as badly as it seems that they will with VAT approximation.

The patchwork of reliefs for charities granted by the UK tax system has developed over time and cannot be said to be the product of a rational application of first principles. However, it has to be admitted that the treatment of charities in this respect is not unique. Although recently there have been attempts at the simplification of charity tax reliefs to make them more understandable by the taxpayer, this has still not been fully achieved. This is probably because it has been done piecemeal and therefore tax simplification has to take place on the macro level and not the micro level.

APPENDIX

THE INCOME TAX SCHEDULES

Schedule	Source	Deductions	Basis of assessment
A	Rents, etc, from land and unfurnished property	Repairs, insurance, services	Net rent due in tax year
D I	profits of trade in UK	Expenses incurred wholly and exclusively for purpose of trade	Adjusted accounts profit for year ending in preceding tax year
D II	Profits of profession or vocation in UK	As D I	As D I
D III	Interest, annuities, annual payments	None	Generally income received in preceding tax year, but major exceptions, eg bank and building society interest
D IV	Foreign securities	None	Income received in preceding tax year
D V	Other foreign possessions	10% deduction against foreign pensions	Income received in preceding tax year
D VI	Income not taxable under other schedules (but limited to certain types)	Varies	Actual income received in tax year
E I, II, III	Offices, employments, pensions, some social security benefits	Expenses incurred wholly, exclusively and necessarily in performance of duties	Actual income received in tax year
F	Dividends and other distributions paid by companies	None	Actual income received in tax year

BIBLIOGRAPHY

Annotated Tax Cases (1922–1975), Vols 1–54 (Gee & Co, London).
Charities and Voluntary Organisations Task Force *Proposals for Reform* (July 1994).
Charity Commission Publications:
    Report of the Charity Commissioners (1980, 1988 and 1990).
    Charities and Fund-raising (CC20) (1996).
    Starting and Registering a Charity (CC21) (1998).
    Choosing and Preparing a Governing Document (CC22) (1999).
    Charities and Trading (CC35) (1995).
    Disaster Appeals: Attorney-General's Guidelines (CC40) (1996).
Chesterman, M *Charities, Trusts and Social Welfare* (Routledge, 1979).
Contributions Agency, *NIC Manual 1 for Employees* (NI 269).
De Voil's Value Added Tax (3 vols) (Simons, 1994).
Farrington, C and Lee, M *Council Tax: Your Guide* (Tolleys, 1993).
Harrison's Inland Revenue Index to Tax Cases, 7th edn (3 vols).
HM Customs & Excise publications:
    Charity advertising and goods connected with collecting donations
    VAT leaflet 700/51 – *VAT Enquiries Guide*
    VAT Leaflet 701/5 – *Clubs and associations*
    VAT Leaflet 701/6 – *Donated medical and scientific equipment*
    VAT Leaflet 701/7 – *Aids for handicapped persons*
    VAT Leaflet 701/28/84 – *Lotteries*
    VAT Leaflet 701/30 – *Education*
    VAT Leaflet 701/41/96 – *Sponsorship*
    VAT Leaflet 708/1 – *Protected buildings*
    VAT Leaflet 708/2 – *Construction industry*
    VAT Leaflet 708/4 – *Construction: VAT certificates for residential or charity buildings*
    VAT Notice 700 – *The VAT guide*
    VAT Notice 700/1/97 – *Should I be registered for VAT?*
    VAT Notice 701/1/95 – *Charities*
    VAT Notice 701/7/94 – *VAT reliefs for people with disabilities*
    VAT Notice 701/59 – *Exemption for fundraising events held by charities and other qualifying bodies*
    VAT Notice 700/2 – *Group Treatment*
    VAT Notice 706 – *Partial exemption*
    VAT Notice 725 – *The Single Market*
    VAT Notice 742A – *Land and property*
Inland Revenue publications:
    IR Charities Series CS2 – *Trading by Charities*
    IR35 *Personal services provided through intermediaries* (March 1999)
    IR64 – Giving to charity – *How businesses get tax relief*
    IR65 – Giving to charity – *How individuals get tax reliefs*
    IR75 – *Tax Reliefs for Charities*
    IR113 – *Gift Aid – A guide for donors and charities*

IR Code of Practice 5 – *Inspection of Charities' Records*

IR ESC C4 – *Fund-Raising for Charity – What to look out for on tax*

IR *Guidance Notes for Charities* (November 2000)

IR *Guidance Notes Getting Britain Giving* (21 March 2000)

Inland Revenue Statistics, various periods, published annually.

Institute of Revenues, Rating and Valuation *Annotated Council Tax and Rating Valuation* (2 vols) (1993).

Jordans Charities Administration Service (Jordans, 2000) edited by Kirkpatrick, P and Randall, A.

Jowitt's Dictionary of English Law, 2nd edn (2 vols) (1977) edited by Burke, J.

Kay, JA and King, MA *The British Tax System* 5th edn (OUP, 1990).

Knight, B Centris Report, *Voluntary Action* (Home Office, 1993).

Laidlow, P *Tax Planning for Post-Death Variations* (Tolleys, 1993).

Law Reports: Statutes, published by the Council of Law Reporting, used for later statutes.

McCluskey, WJ and Moss PJ *The Uniform Business Rate* (Tolleys, 1992).

McCutcheon, BD and Waterhouse, C *McCutcheon on Inheritance Tax* 3rd edn (1988).

Mitchell, K *Trading by Charities* (CTRG, 1994).

Noakes, P *VAT Planning* (Tolleys, 1993).

Ryde on Rating and the Council Tax (2 vols), 8th and 13th edns (Simons, 1994).

Stewart, C and Reynolds, S *A Guide to the Council Tax* (1993).

Tax Case Reports (1875–2000), Vols 1–72 (The Stationery Office)

Terra, BJM and Kajus, J *A Guide to the European VAT Directives* (4 vols) (1993).

VAT Tribunal Reports, 1973–, Crown Copyright.

Venables, R and Kessler, J *Tax Planning and Fundraising for Charities* (Keyhaven, 1994).

Whitehouse, C and Stuart-Buttle, E *Revenue Law* (FT Pearson, 1993).

INDEX

References are to paragraph numbers, addendum to Chapter 10, and Appendix.